ISBN 978-0-282-00824-6
PIBN 10838277

1 MONTH OF
FREE
READING

at

www.ForgottenBooks.com

By purchasing this book you are eligible for one month membership to ForgottenBooks.com, giving you unlimited access to our entire collection of over 1,000,000 titles via our web site and mobile apps.

To claim your free month visit:

www.forgottenbooks.com/free838277

English
Français
Deutsche
Italiano
Español
Português

www.forgottenbooks.com

Mythology Photography **Fiction**
Fishing Christianity **Art** Cooking
Essays Buddhism Freemasonry
Medicine **Biology** Music **Ancient
Egypt** Evolution Carpentry Physics
Dance Geology **Mathematics** Fitness
Shakespeare **Folklore** Yoga Marketing
Confidence Immortality Biographies
Poetry **Psychology** Witchcraft
Electronics Chemistry History **Law**
Accounting **Philosophy** Anthropology
Alchemy Drama Quantum Mechanics
Atheism Sexual Health **Ancient History**
Entrepreneurship Languages Sport
Paleontology Needlework Islam
Metaphysics Investment Archaeology
Parenting Statistics Criminology
Motivational

THE CASE FOR PIRIT PHOTOGRAPHY

BY

ARTHUR CONAN DOYLE

WITH CORROBORATIVE EVIDENCE BY
EXPERIENCED RESEARCHERS
AND PHOTOGRAPHERS

ILLUSTRATED

NEW YORK
GEORGE H. DORAN COMPANY

PREFACE

THE publicity given to the recent attacks on Psychic Photography has been out of all proportion to their scientific value as evidence. When Sir Arthur Conan Doyle returned to Great Britain, after his successful tour in America, the controversy was in full swing. With characteristic promptitude he immediately decided to meet these negative attacks by a positive counter-attack, and this volume is the outcome of that decision.

We have used the term "Spirit Photography" on the title-page as being the popular name by which these phenomena are known. This does not imply that either Sir Arthur or I imagine that everything supernormal must be of spirit origin. There is, undoubtedly, a broad borderland where these photographic effects may be produced from forces contained within ourselves. This merges into those higher phenomena of which many cases are here described. Those desiring fuller information on this subject are referred to "Photographing the Invisible," by James Coates.

It was only when editing the matter for these pages that I fully realised what an overwhelming mass of reliable material we had to work upon. In restricting this book to the necessary limits it has only been possible to make use of a small portion of this evidence. Many more cases have been placed on record and may be published on some future occasion. Most of the

PREFACE

letters accompanying these descriptions display a deep and genuine affection for the maligned mediums of the Crewe Circle. Our hearty thanks are due to all those friends who have so readily co-operated in this work and who are so willing to brave the discomforts of publicity for what they know to be the truth.

FRED BARLOW.

CONTENTS

ILLUSTRATIONS

[ix]

ILLUSTRATIONS

THE CASE FOR
SPIRIT PHOTOGRAPHY

THE CASE FOR
SPIRIT PHOTOGRAPHY

CHAPTER I

THE CREWE CIRCLE

AN accusation of a damaging, and, as I believe, of an entirely unfounded character, has been brought forward by Mr. Harry Price against Mr. Hope, whose name has for more than seventeen years been associated with the strange phenomenon which has been called spirit photography. I will deal later with this accusation with which the Society for Psychic Research has unfortunately associated itself by publishing the report of it in their official journal. Before touching upon it I should wish to take a broader sweep and to show the overpowering weight of evidence which exists as to the reality of Mr. Hope's most remarkable gift.

If a man were accused of cowardice it would be natural that his defender should not confine himself to the particular case, but should examine the man's whole career and put forward instances of valour as an argument against the charge. So also if a man is accused of dishonesty a long record of honesty would be his most complete defence. Therefore in considering the case of Mr. Hope, and the value of his mediumship, one must not limit one's investigation to a single case, where errors of observation and of deduction may creep in, but must take a broader view which will embrace an account of a long series of cases, vouched for by men and women of the highest character, and incompatible with any form of fraud. If the reader will have the patience to follow my facts and my argument, I hope to make it clear to any unprejudiced mind that there is overwhelming evidence that we have in Mr. Hope a man endowed with most singular powers, and that, instead of persecuting and misrepresenting him, it would be wiser if we took a sympathetic view of his remarkable work, which has brought consolation to the afflicted, and conviction to many who had lost all belief in the independent life of the spirit.

Many speak of Mr. Hope and of the Crewe Circle without any definite idea of what the words mean. Let me explain, then, that Mr. William Hope, who is a working-man, discovered, some seventeen years ago, quite by chance, that this remarkable power of producing extra faces, figures or objects upon photographic plates had been given to him. In the first instance he was taking a fellow-workman, and the plate, when developed, was found to contain an extra figure which was recognised as being a likeness of his comrade's sister, who had recently passed away.

This form of mediumship is rare, but from the days of Mumler, who first showed it in 1861, there has never been a time when one or more sensitives have not been able to demonstrate it.

Hope was greatly surprised at his own results, but he had the good fortune in early days to meet the late

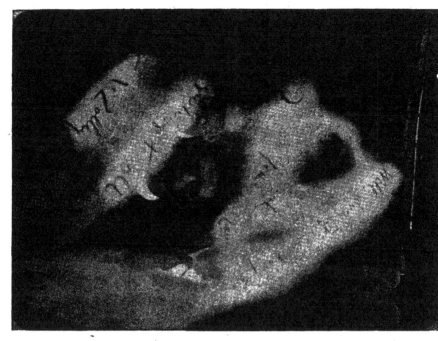

Fig. 1.—Impression received upon a marked plate which never left the author's hands, save when in carrier. (*See* p. 21.)

Fig. 2.—Specimen of Archdeacon Colley's writing during his lifetime. (*See* p. 22.)

FIG. 3.—Psychograph in the handwriting of
Dr. W. J. Crawford. (*See* p. 25.)

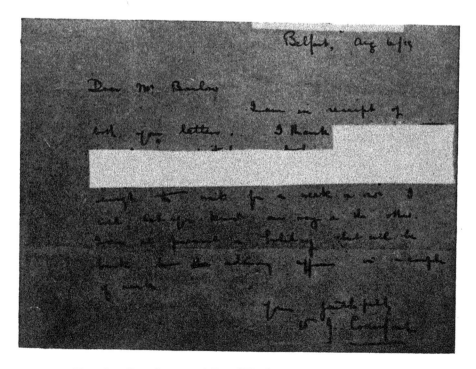

FIG. 4.—Specimen of Dr. W. J. Crawford's writing
during his lifetime.

THE CREWE CIRCLE

Archdeacon Colley, an enlightened member of the Anglican Church, who tested his powers, endorsed them and appreciated their value. It was he who gave Hope his first stand camera, the old-fashioned instrument to which he still clings, and which, with its battered box and broken leg, is familiar to many of us.

No one knows the story of these beginnings so well as Miss Scatcherd, who was the intimate friend of the Archdeacon and shared the evidence which had so impressed him. Miss Scatcherd has kindly consented to jot down her reminiscences of these early days, that I may include them in the later pages of this volume.

Suffice it if I say, at present, that Hope has been before the public for seventeen years, that during that time many special tests have been demanded of him and have been successfully met, that he has been closely observed by experts of all sorts—scientific men (including Sir William Crookes), journalists, professional photographers and others—that he has patiently submitted himself to all sorts of experiment, and that he has emerged from this most drastic ordeal with the complete support and approval of far the greater part of his clients. That he has been fiercely attacked goes without saying, for every medium has that experience, but each fresh allegation against him has ended in smoke, while his gifts have grown stronger with time, so that the percentage of blanks in his results is, I should say, lower than it used to be. No medium can ever honestly guarantee success, but it would probably be within the mark if one claimed that Hope attained it three times out of five, though the results vary much in visibility and value, being mere vague

[15]

outlines in some cases, and in others so detailed in their perfection that the extra is clearer and more lifelike than the sitter. These variations seem to depend upon the state of health of the medium, the qualities of the investigator, the atmospheric conditions and other obscure causes.

In person, Hope is a man who gives the impression of being between fifty and sixty years of age, with the manner and appearance of an intelligent working-man. His forehead is high and indicates a good, if untrained, brain beneath it. The general effect of his face is aquiline with large, well-opened, honest blue eyes, and a moustache which is shading from yellow to grey. His voice is pleasant, with a North Country accent which becomes very pronounced when he is excited. His hands with their worn nails and square-ended fingers are those of the worker, and the least adapted to sleight-of-hand tricks of any that I have seen.

Mrs. Buxton, who aids him, is a kindly, pleasant-faced woman on the sunny side of middle-age. Her mediumistic powers seem to be akin to those of Hope, and though the latter had all his earlier results independently, he is stronger when he combines his forces with Mrs. Buxton's.

They both give an impression of honesty and frankness, which increases as one comes to know them more closely. I have never met two people who seemed to me from manner and appearance to be less likely to be in a conspiracy to deceive the public.

They and all their circle are spiritualists of a Salvation Army type, much addicted to the hearty singing of hymns and the putting up of impromptu prayers.

Hope, the most unconventional of beings, has been known in the midst of one of his photographic lectures (which he delivers occasionally in his shirt-sleeves) to say, "And now, my friends, we will warm up with a hymn," in which the audience, unable to escape, has to acquiesce. It is a type of character which associates itself sometimes, I admit, with a loathsome form of hypocrisy, but which has in it something peculiarly childlike and sweet when it is perfectly honest and spontaneous as it is, to the best of my belief, in the case of the two mediums in question.

Some prejudice can be excited against Hope by the mere assertion that he is a professional medium. The public is aware that fraud—sometimes unhappily real, sometimes only alleged—is too often associated with this profession. Sufficient allowance is not made for the fact that the papers only take note of psychic things when they go wrong, and never when they go right. The dishonest medium is so easily found out that one could hardly make a living at so precarious a trade.

In a very extended experience, which covers many hundreds of séances, I have only encountered fraud three or four times. Had I registered those cases and omitted the others, I would have given the impression of continued fraud, which is exactly how the matter is presented to the public who are continually hood-winked, not by the spiritualists but by the critics and so-called "exposers" who represent what is exceptional as being constant.

It is exactly this prejudice which prevents a medium or his friends from bringing an action for libel, so that the unhappy man or woman becomes a butt for any charge or any ridicule, the assailants knowing well that the ordinary legal rights of a Briton are hardly applicable to one who can be represented as living from a profession which is not recognised by our laws. This cowardly medium-baiting will cease only when the public show, by abstaining from the purchase of the journals which pursue it, that they have no sympathy with such persecutions.

I would wish to point out, however, that Hope is not in a strict sense a professional medium. I have never met anyone who seemed to me less venal than he. I am aware of a case where an exploiter approached him with a proposal to turn his gift into money, but was received in the coldest possible manner. Twice when I have sat with him at Crewe he has refused to take a fee, though he could never have known that the fact would be made public. It is true that on each occasion I disregarded him to the extent of leaving some remembrance upon the mantelpiece when his back was turned, but I have been assured by others that he has again and again refused all remuneration for his sitting, and has charged the ridiculous sum of 4s. 6d. per dozen for prints from the negatives obtained. This sum is calculated upon the average time expended at the rate of his own trade earnings. I do not wish to overstate this side of the question or to pretend that he would not be open to a present from a grateful client. Of how many of us could that be honestly said? But my point is that his gifts have been as open to the poor as to the rich—which all spiritual gifts should be.

It is, of course, another matter when he comes to London and gives sittings by appointment at the British

College of Psychic Science. That college is an expensive and most useful establishment, which is run, with a yearly deficit, through the generosity of Mr. and Mrs. Hewat McKenzie, and it is only right that those who use it should contribute an adequate sum to its maintenance.

To illustrate my remarks upon Hope's character and the general lines upon which the Crewe Circle is conducted, I would like to give this extract from the letter of a miner, Mr. East, of 36, New Street, Port Talbot, who describes an experience which he had in 1920. After giving an account of the precautions taken, and of the appearance upon the plate of his son's face: [*See* Figure IL]

"Hundreds of persons who knew him have seen the photo and recognised him." He adds: "When I asked what their charges were, Mr. Hope replied: 'Four and sixpence a dozen. For the sitting, nothing. This is a gift from God and we dare not charge for what is freely given us. Our pay is often the wonder and joy depicted on the faces of those, like yourselves, who have found that their loved ones are not entirely lost to them. We get all kinds and classes of people here. Some even are threadbare and too poor to pay train-fare, but we treat them all alike as we recognise in each a brother or sistèr.'

"I could not but be impressed by the Christ-spirit of the two friends, whom we had never seen before that short half-hour, and not since. And when I read of men who try to make those two persons appear something detestable I go back in memory to that day when it was our good fortune to meet them and recall their more than kind attitude to two bruised hearts. God bless them, say I."

THE CASE FOR SPIRIT PHOTOGRAPHY

With these preliminary remarks I will now lay before the reader a selection of cases which I have taken from Mr. Hope's record, and I will ask him to read them carefully and see if they can be reconciled with any possible system of fraud. We are, of course, always open to the objection that a man may be perfectly honest fifty times and fraudulent the fifty-first. That is undeniable and constitutes the great difficulty in dealing with isolated cases where no impartial witness was present, and where both the accusation and the defence are equally *ex-parte* statements. We can only say in rebuttal that previous honesty must predispose us to assume that there is no fraud, and remind our readers that if we can only show one single case, which is absolutely beyond criticism, then we have for ever settled the larger contention, that it is possible in the presence of certain individuals, whom we call mediums, to produce effects which are super-normal and which would appear to indicate separate intelligences acting visibly quite independently of ourselves.

CHAPTER II

I WILL first give an account of my own visit to Crewe which was in the summer of 1919. I bought my plates in Manchester and then travelled over to keep the appointment which had been made a week before. Arriving at Crewe, I went down to the little house in Market Street, which is so modest and humble that it furnishes an argument in itself against any undue cupidity on the part of its tenant. Two spiritualistic friends, Mr. Oaten, editor of the *Two Worlds,* and Mr. Walker, were my companions.

Mr. Hope and Mrs. Buxton were waiting for us, and, after a short religious service, Mr. Hope and I went into the dark room. There I opened the packet of plates, put two into the carrier and marked them then and there. The carrier was then taken into the room and Mr. Hope inserted it into the camera. We three spiritualists sat in front with a rug, or blanket, as a background. The exposure having been made, the carrier was taken back into the dark room where, with my own hands, I took out the plates, developed them and fixed them. So far as I could judge, there was at no stage any possibility of changing the plates.

But this question does not really arise. No changing of plates would account for the effect actually produced. This effect I have shown in Figure 1. There is a hazy cloud covering us of what I will describe as ectoplasm, though my critics are very welcome to call it cotton-wool if it eases their feelings to do so. In one corner appears a partial materialisation of what seems to be the hair and forehead of a young man. Across the plate is scrawled, "Well done, Friend Doyle, I welcome you to Crewe. Greetings to all. T. COLLEY."

I have already explained that Archdeacon Colley was the founder of the Crewe Circle, and if, as we believe, we continue our interest after death it would seem not unnatural that he should send a kindly word to a visitor who was working for the cause. How can we determine that the message was really from Archdeacon Colley? The obvious way would be to get a sample of his writing in life and to compare it with that upon the plate. This I have done, as shown in Figure 2. Can anyone deny that the handwriting is the same in both instances, or can anyone suppose that the rough script of Hope could possibly be modified into the scholarly handwriting of the Archdeacon? Whence, then, did this message come? Does anyone imagine that a private forger is retained by Hope and lurks somewhere in that humble abode? It is a problem which calls for an answer, and no talk about conjuring tricks or transposition of plates has the least bearing upon it. It may be remarked incidentally that my own strong desire was to obtain some sign from my son who had passed away the year before. The result seemed to show that our personal wishes do not effect the outcome.

Having failed to get what I desired, I remained at Crewe for the night, and next morning went down to Market Street again. On this occasion I used Hope's own plates, having left mine at the hotel. He gave me the choice of several packets. The result obtained under all the precautions which I could adopt (it would only weary the reader if I gave every point of detail) was a photograph of the face of a young man beside my own. It was not a good likeness of my son, though it resembled him as he was some eight years before his death. Of the three results which I obtained at Crewe it was the one which impressed me least. On examination with a lens it was noticeable that the countenance was pitted with fine dots, as in the case of process printing. This is to be noticed in a certain proportion, possibly one in ten, of Hope's results, and occurs in the case of persons whose faces could by no possibility have appeared in newspapers. One can only suppose that it is in some way connected with the psychic process, and some have imagined a reticulated screen upon which the image is built up. I am content to note the fact without attempting to explain it. I have observed the same effect in other psychic photographs.

The third result was the most remarkable of any. I had read that Hope can get images without the use of the camera, but the statement sounded incredible. He now asked me to mark a plate and put it in a carrier, which I did. We then placed our hands on either side of the carrier, Mrs. Buxton and her sister joining in. At the end of about a minute Hope gave a sort of shudder, and intimated that he thought a result had been obtained. On putting the plate into the solution a disc the size of a shilling, perfectly black, sprang up in the centre of it. On development this resolved itself into a luminous circle with the face of a female delicately outlined within it. Under the chin is a disc of white, and two fingers which are pointing to it. The disc is evidently a brooch, and the pointing seemed to indicate that it was meant to be evidential. The face bore a strong resemblance to that of my elder sister, who died some thirty years ago. Upon sending the print to my other sisters they not only confirmed this, but they reminded me that my sister had a very remarkable ivory brooch in her lifetime and that it was just the one object which might best have been chosen as a test. I regret that this picture is so delicate that it will not bear reproduction.

Such were my three results at Crewe, and I should, I hold, have been devoid of reason had I not been deeply impressed by them. Here was a message in Archdeacon Colley's own handwriting. Here was a test from my own dead sister which seemed to be beyond all possible coincidence, apart from the extraordinary way in which the picture was obtained. Neither sleight-of-hand nor transference of plates could have any bearing upon such results as those. Their full significance was not realised until I had made enquiries, but after that time I felt it impossible to doubt the super-normal nature of the powers which had produced such effects.

It might perhaps be argued that as Archdeacon Colley's writing was familiar to Hope, he had, in spite of his disabilities, made some special effort to master and reproduce it. As a matter of fact, however, this case does not stand alone, and many evidential writings have been obtained at Crewe, notably those of W. T. Stead and of the late Dr. Crawford. The latter is a recent incident, and I would take it as my next example, since it illustrates this phenomenon of writing, and is again free from the bogey of transposition.

Upon June 30 of this year (1922) three delegates from Belfast, Mr. Skelton, Mr. Gillmour and Mr. Donaldson, were coming over to the London Spiritualists' Conference. They broke their journey at Crewe in order to have a sitting with Mr. Hope, who was in deep distress at the time on account of the attack made upon him in Mr. Price's report. It is worth noting that Mrs. Crawford, the widow of Dr. Crawford, had come over with them on the boat, and that Dr. Crawford's affairs had been under discussion, though Hope had no means of knowing it. Under good fraud-proof conditions, on their own specially-marked plate, the visitors obtained a message in Dr. Crawford's handwriting, which runs thus, I supplying the punctuation:

"DEAR MR. HOPE,

"Needless to say I am with you where psychic work is concerned, and you can be sure of my sympathy and help. I know all the difficulties and uncertainties connected with the subject. I am keenly interested in your circle and will co-operate with you. Regarding your enemies who would by hook or by crook dispose of the phenomena, leave them alone. I, W. J. Crawford, of Belfast, am here in Crewe on Friday, June 30th.

"W. J. CRAWFORD."

Each word is on its own little patch of ectoplasm, or upon its own pad of cotton-wool, if the critics prefer it, though it would puzzle them, I think, to reproduce the effect which is given in Figure 3. The plate alongside (Figure 4) shows a reproduction of an actual note of Crawford's which will enable the reader to judge the extreme similarity of the script. Once more we confront the critic with this fact and ask him to face the difficulty and to tell us whence this writing came; whether it is a production of Mr. Hope's, or whether the theory of a private forger upon the premises can be sustained.

Apart from these cases of the reproduction of handwriting, copies of documents have appeared upon the plates at Crewe which could by no means have got there in a normal fashion. A case in point is given in detail by the Reverend and venerable Professor Henslow on p. 217 of his *Proofs of Spiritualism*. In this case, the truth of which is vouched for by the Professor, although it did not actually occur to him, the plates were held between the hands of the sitters in the manner already described, but the packet had not been opened and was as it had come from the chemist. When the packet was opened and the plates developed there was found impressed upon the fifth plate a number of Greek characters, which proved to be a copy of four lines of the *Codex Alexandrinus*, a rare Greek text kept in a glass case in the British Museum. The interesting point appears that the two documents are not facsimiles, and that there is some slight difference in the formation of the letters, thus meeting the objection that the text photographed might have been got from some facsimile of the original *Codex*. The photographs of the original Greek and of the Crewe reproduction are given in Professor Henslow's work. Here, again, we may well ask the critic to face the facts and to give us some feasible explanation as to how this Greek text was precipitated on to a plate in a sealed packet under the mediumship of an unlearned carpenter at Crewe.

CHAPTER III

WE will now turn to the reproduction of faces, and I will give an instance where all the stock theories about changing or superposition of plates become untenable. At the annual meeting of the Society for the Study of Supernormal Pictures, I being present, a photograph of the members was taken in the normal way as a souvenir. As Hope was present, it was suggested that a second photograph be taken by him in the hope that we might get some psychic effect. The plate was taken from an unopened packet in the pocket of the secretary, and some fifteen of us were witnesses of the whole transaction. Hope had no warning at all, and could have made no preparation. The plate was at once developed by one of our own members, and a well-marked extra, amid a cloud of ectoplasm, appeared upon the picture. This extra was claimed by one of our members as a good likeness of his dead father. This result, which is illustrated by Figure 5, was obtained before an audience of experts, if any men in this world have a right to call themselves experts upon this subject. How can it be explained by fraud and how can such a case be lightly set aside? Granting for argument's sake that the sitter may have been

[28]

mistaken in the recognition, how can the actual psychic effect be accounted for?

It happens, occasionally, that these ghost-faces which appear upon the plates retain some remarkable physical peculiarity which prove beyond all question who they represent. One such case has been handed to me by the Countess of Malmesbury, whose own account is so clear and condensed that it could not be bettered:

"I sat with Mr. Hope and Mrs. Buxton on Friday, December 9th, 1921, and was accompanied by 'Val L'Estrange,' a lady professional photographer, who watched the proceedings on my behalf, as I do not understand photography. She states that from first to last she could not detect any fraud. As I sat for the photograph the wish just crossed my mind that I might obtain a photograph of J. H., who died in 1880, and that I could receive a definite sign that it was genuine.

"J. H. died as the result of an operation for the removal of the lower jaw, which had been seriously injured. No one saw him after this terrible misfortune except five persons, of whom I am the only survivor, and I need not say that no photograph was then taken of him.

"I showed the photograph to Dr. Fielding Ould, who at once recognised it as that of a man who had had his lower jaw removed. This opinion was confirmed by several of his medical friends, to whom he showed the picture.

"I should add that the plates were bought by 'Val L'Estrange' direct from the manufacturer, and that we brought them with us. The exposure was forty seconds. The plate which produced the portrait was manipulated by Mr. Hope under the supervision of 'Val L'Estrange.' We both superintended the development and fixing of the negative.

THE CASE FOR SPIRIT PHOTOGRAPHY

"As an impartial investigator of psychic matters I have stated exactly what took place, without comment.

(*signed*) SUSAN, COUNTESS OF MALMESBURY."

It must be admitted that this case, so exactly recorded, would be a difficult one to explain away.

I would now quote the case furnished by Major Spencer, who is an experienced and careful observer, and has given much attention to psychic photography. In this experiment he used his own camera, his own carriers and his own plates. What could be more drastic than that! He says, if I may abbreviate his account:

"The box of plates was never out of my sight and was cut open in the dark room by myself; Hope or Mrs. Buxton in no instance touching them."

The red light, he explains, was a good one and he could see all that occurred.

"Hope stood on my left hand for the whole time in the dark room and I kept the box of plates under my right elbow during the operations of initialling and inserting the plates in the slides. . . . My own camera remained closed in my despatch-case (also closed) till I returned from the dark room, when I set it up on its tripod, extending it, and focussing it upon the chair afterwards used. When the exposures were made by Hope I had to explain to him how to actuate the shutter, as the lever on the camera front was new to him. The only contact with the camera was when he touched this lever. Exposure thirty-five seconds. Neither Mrs. Buxton nor Hope knew that I had intended using my own camera and dark slides till we met in the studio. These slides are metallic and each contains one plate."

[30]

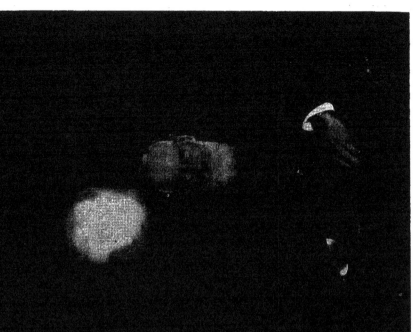

FIG. 7.—Sir William Crookes with psychic face obtained in his own laboratory through the mediumship of the Crewe Circle. (*See* p. 33.)

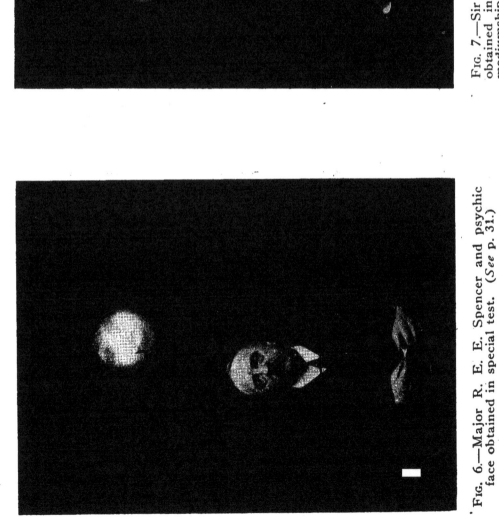

FIG. 6.—Major R. E. E. Spencer and psychic face obtained in special test. (*See* p. 31.)

(For the benefit of the uninitiated, let me explain that the carrier and the dark slide are different names for the same thing, the receptacle into which the plates are put in the dark room, which is then inserted into the back of the camera.)

Now this is a case which any reasonable man would say eliminated every possible source of error. The actual result was that out of six plates, two showed unrecognised extra faces. One of the results is reproduced in Figure 6. How came those faces upon the plates? How can our critics explain it? They cannot explain it, and yet they have not the honesty to admit their inability. Among our chief enemies is that inner circle which for the moment controls the destinies of the Society for Psychical Research. What flaw do they find? I am sure the honest common-sense reader would never guess. The flaw adduced is that Major Spencer left his camera inside his despatch-box in the studio while he was in the dark room. Mrs. Buxton was in the studio. She might have dashed at the box, pulled it open, dragged out the camera, and then . . . well, what then? No one can imagine what the next stage would be. Dr. Abraham Wallace has publicly asked the critic to state what could then be done which would have put two human faces upon different plates and none on the others. If Major Spencer had locked his box it would then have been claimed that Mrs. Buxton had a skeleton key in her pocket. It is puerile criticism of this sort which has lowered that intellectual respect which we older members had once for the S.P.R. It is intellectually dishonest and the sign of a frame of mind which is not there to follow facts or to ascertain the truth, but only to argue a preconceived case as a lawyer speaks from his brief. The S.P.R. (or their present spokesmen) are against psychic photography, and therefore it is better to put up the most childish and preposterous objections rather than to say that a case is clearly proved. I would appeal to any impartial mind whether this case of Major Spencer's does not absolutely cover every objection.

I would now give the case of the dream-hand of Lady Grey of Falloden. When I was going to Australia this lady most kindly wrote out the facts for me and gave me a copy of the photograph, which I used upon my screen. Lady Glenconner, as she then was, dreamed that if she was photographed at Crewe she would see her son's hand resting upon her left shoulder. She said nothing to Hope, but she put the fact of her dream upon record. Sure enough, in the photograph there is a small cloud of ectoplasm, and emerging from it a hand, which is resting even as it rested in the dream. Where does fraud come in, in such a case as that? Surely those who circulated a libellous pamphlet against Hope upon the strength of a single case must feel ashamed when they consider such a result as that, where no possible manipulation could have affected the picture. Psychic caution is an admirable quality, but extreme incredulity is even more disastrous than extreme credulity. The psychic investigator should be a filter, not a block.

I would now quote the case of Mr. Pearse, a well-known business man of Manchester. This is no psychic fanatic, but a hard-headed Northern man of business.

He visited Hope at Crewe, taking with him his own
new camera and his own carrier, which was loaded by
his daughter. No chance of transposition here, unless
Hope had a duplicate carrier.

"The result," he says, "was an undisputed likeness
to my father. *No photograph of him in that position
is in existence.* Everyone who has known him has
recognised him, and my mother treasures the photograph very much."

In this account the sting lies in the statement that
no such photograph is in existence. Again and again—
it would not be too much to say that fifty instances could
be produced—this statement can be made. Is it not
incredible that people should be found who cannot see
that such a fact is evidential of supernormal action?

I have alluded to the fact that Sir William Crookes
received such a photograph at Crewe, and that it bore
a close resemblance to his deceased wife. I have not
been able to get any copy of this photograph, but it is
devoutly to be hoped that it, and Sir William's invalu-
able psychic papers, are being duly cared for by his
executors and biographer, for they have there a precious
trust, and any tampering with it on account of their
individual opinions would entail upon them the censure
of generations yet unborn. In an interview in the
Christian Commonwealth (December 4th, 1918) the in-
terviewer, Miss Scatcherd, asked, "And may I say
how you went north with another friend and myself
and procured on your own marked plate, under your
own conditions, a likeness of your beloved wife, the late
Lady Crookes?" To which Sir William answered:

[33]

Figure 8

THE CASE FOR SPIRIT PHOTOGRAPHY

"You may say that, since it is the truth. . . . You may
add that the picture obtained after her passing on is
unlike any of the many which I possess, but certainly
resembles my dear one in her last days of failing
health." In a private letter, which I have seen, Sir William, writing on December 14, 1916, shortly after the
incident, says: "The photograph is easily recognised
by all to whom I have shown it. I find that it is very
similar in likeness to one I took about ten years ago,
although by no means a facsimile reproduction. This
makes it all the more satisfactory to me."

Though I am unable to reproduce this photograph,
I have been able, by the kindness of Miss Scatcherd, to
reproduce (Figure 7) the preliminary experimental
photograph got in Sir William's laboratory, which
induced him to take the Crewe Circle seriously. Only
Mr. Hope and Miss Scatcherd were present on this
occasion. It was taken, says the latter, "under the
strictest conditions that the genius of Sir William
Crookes, backed by his unusual common sense, could
suggest." The face here is not that of Lady Crookes,
and was not recognised. But surely such a result must
show the public how superficial is the view which on
the strength of a single experiment endeavours to discredit the whole life's work of Mr. Hope.

Several examples of Crewe photographs are reproduced (Figures 8, 9, 10) which show the similarity
to the living man, and yet are declared by the relatives to be unlike any existing picture. That which
is shown on Figure 8 is the result obtained by that
brave psychic pioneer, the Rev. Charles Tweedale, who
from his little Yorkshire vicarage beckons the Church

[34]

on the road that it should go. In this case Mr. Tweedale called upon Hope without any appointment and
obtained, as has several times been obtained on surprise visits, an excellent result. The psychic face is
that of his wife's father, whose features in life, for
purposes of comparison, are shown by Figure 9. The
picture is unlike any in existence.

I have said that the psychic faces are sometimes more
animated and lifelike than the original photographs
taken in life. In support of this assertion I would point
to Figure 10. The old man who smiles so happily is
Mrs. Buxton's own father, then very recently dead.
I do not think that the most cynical of my readers will
contend that a daughter is likely to make a blasphemous
faked picture of her own father, even if it had been
possible to produce so vital an effect.

Anyone who is familiar with Hope's results is aware
that over many of the psychic faces there appears a roll
or arch of some peculiar substance which has never
been explained upon any supposition of fraud, but is
so constant that it would appear to be part of the psychic
process. Some of us have always contended that probably this arch represents a formation corresponding to
the Cabinet upon this side—an envelope or enclosed
space within which psychic forces are generated and
condensed. The arch is by no means peculiar to Hope,
though the exact form and texture of it is such that one
could pick out a Hope photograph among a hundred
others. This psychic arch, as it has been named, appears in many forms and many places, some of them
very unexpected. I have, as an example, a photograph
before me as I write which was taken by Mr. Boyd, the

[35]

respected provost of a Scotch borough, upon a recent journey which he made upon the West Coast of Africa. On taking a small group of natives he found an extra of a woman and child (negroes) upon his plate. This extra figure is surrounded and surmounted by the psychic arch in an exaggerated form. Mr. Boyd has no axe to grind, and, so far as I know, he is not even a spiritualist. How comes it, then, that his result fits so definitely into the arch system, if it be not that there is some general law which regulates results whether they be obtained in Crewe or on the Gold Coast?

Again, I have a friend, an amateur, who has himself developed psychic photography from the time that it was a mere luminous blur upon his plates, until now he receives very graceful and perfect pictures which are in some cases recognised faces of the dead. In his case the arch adjusts itself into the form of an artistic hood or mantilla. But the arch principle carries on. It is only by a comprehensive view of this sort, and by the comparison of different independent results, that we are likely to get at some of the laws which underlie this matter. At present the system adopted in quarters which should be responsible ones is to concentrate attention upon whatever may seem to be failure or deception, and to take no notice at all of the broader aspects of the question. In every science the methods of advance are to pay strict attention to the positive results and to regard the negative ones as mere warnings of what to avoid. This process has been reversed in considering psychic photography, and the world has been deceived by those who should have been its guides. Truth will, of course, prevail, but its progress has been grievously retarded by this unhappy and unscientific mental attitude.

On one occasion remarkable evidence was afforded that we were right in our surmise that a cabinet of ectoplasm for concentration is first constructed, and that the psychic effect is developed inside it. The result, which is depicted in Figure 12, was got by Mr. Jeffrey, of Glasgow, who was, I may add, the President of the Scottish Society of Magicians, and is therefore the last person to be deceived by any sort of trick. In this case the exposure seems to have been too early so that the ectoplasmic bag is exposed in its complete form, without any contents. In the second picture, Figure 13, taken immediately afterwards, the face of Mr. Jeffrey's deceased wife has appeared, and the bag has split to show it, forming the familiar fold over both sides of the face. This picture seems to me to be quite final in showing us exactly how the matter is worked by the forces which direct things upon the other side.

Each of these cases which I have given is impressive, I hope, in itself, but their cumulative effect should be overpowering. They are but selections out of a very long list which I could provide, but repetition would be unprofitable, for if those which are here quoted fail to convince the reader then he is surely beyond conviction. One or two might conceivably be the result of imperfect observation or incorrect statement, but it is an insult to common sense to say that so long an array of honourable witnesses, with their precise detail, with their actual photographic results, and with the complete exclusion of any possible trickery, should all be explained in any normal fashion.

CHAPTER IV

AN EXAMINATION OF MR. HOPE AND HIS CRITICS

HAVING said so much in support of Mr. Hope's mediumship, let me say what I can in the way of personal criticism, for I hold no particular brief for him, and am only anxious to follow truth wherever it may lead. I have written this pamphlet because I think that truth has been grievously obscured, and that the fruit of seventeen years of remarkable psychic demonstration is, for the moment, imperilled by the attention of the public being directed entirely to a single case which is, admittedly upon the face of it, of a damaging character. We spiritualists should be, in Stevenson's fine phrase, "steel-true and blade-straight," and we should never avoid an issue, or fall into the error of our opponents who have no sense of balance and can only focus their gaze upon one side of a question.

It has been said that Hope is suspiciously restless and fussy in the dark room. This, so far as my own observation goes, is correct. It may be that he is nervously anxious for success, or it may be that he is not in a normal condition—for he usually holds a service and occasionally goes into apparent trance immediately before the experiment. Whatever the cause, I am not prepared to deny the fact, or that not unreasonable suspicions might be awakened by his attitude in the minds of those who are brought for the first time in

AN EXAMINATION OF MR. HOPE

contact with his personality. I can only point to the cases already given, and say once more that *no* action upon his part could have produced them.

Again, it is said of Hope that he is impatient of tests and restrictions. Some of his best friends have been alienated by this fact. Mediums are touchy people— more delicately organised in many cases than any other human type. They may occasionally show an irrational annoyance and resentment against any action which implies personal suspicion. And yet, though he certainly prefers to be left to his own methods unrestrained save by ordinary observation, it is a fact that he has in the past consented to a great number of tests and has come out of them remarkably well. I have heard him say, "What have I to gain from tests? I am put to a deal of trouble, I do what I am asked to do, I get result, and then I hear no more about it except that perhaps I have convinced the person. Or perhaps, even if I have done all he asks in his own way, he still says he is unconvinced." I can bear him out in this latter statement, for I have knowledge of three separate sittings which he had with a well-known London editor, where, under the latter's ever more stringent conditions, Hope got results certainly twice, and, I think, thrice, and yet when I asked this editor to vouch for these results that I might quote them in this pamphlet, in the interests of truth and justice, I could get no reply to my letter. This seems to indicate either that he was not yet satisfied, though his own conditions had been carried out, or else that he had not the moral courage to help the medium at the time when he needed testimony.

The incident shows that there is some truth in Hope's

[39]

contention that tests are often a waste of energy. At the same time, it should be known that when the S.P.R. made their recent attack, founded upon a single case, Hope at once offered to give fresh sittings and to submit to the most drastic tests so long as those who were in sympathy were also associated in the experiment. For some reason the S.P.R. refused this, and it is a serious flaw in their position. None the less, we must make the admission that, in general, Hope is not fond of tests.

But there is another and more serious admission which I would make, although in doing so I may possibly be doing Hope an injustice. He is, in my opinion, not only a spiritualist, but a fanatic, which is a dangerous thing in any line of thought. We are aware that one must "test the spirits," but I believe that Hope has such childlike and blind faith in his guides that he would obey their directions whatever they might be. I recollect one case where a distinguished man of science sent Hope a sealed packet, upon which the latter placed it in a bucket of water, under the alleged prompting of some spirit message. The natural result was to alienate the scientific man from psychic photography for many years. It is easy to say that this was simply a case of vulgar fraud, but fraud would be done in some manner which could be concealed and not in so drastic a manner as that, and, as I have shown, fraud does not at all fit in with Hope's usual results. I make the critic a present of the case, merely adding that I believe Hope's account of his motives to be absolutely true, however incomprehensible it might seem.

I have now, I hope, convinced any reasonable reader of the genuine nature of Hope's powers, which, after all, wonderful as they may seem, are by no means unique, but are to be matched by those of several contemporaries both in England and in America—not all of them professionals.

We will next turn to the particular case treated in the report of the S.P.R. drawn up by Mr. Price, and afterwards published in a sixpenny form and widely distributed gratis with the evident intention of ruining Hope. Apart from its truth or falseness, the pamphlet is in deplorable taste, with puns upon Hope's name, and tags of Johnson and Dryden dotted over it. So grave a subject should be treated with dignity even when severity is necessary. I will now state the case as clearly as I can, together with some remarkable sidelights which have appeared since the publication.

Having determined to catch Hope out, Mr. Price, who has considerable knowledge both of conjuring and of photography, procured from the Imperial Dry Plate Company eight plates, all of which had been cut from the same sheet of glass. Six of these plates were made up into a single packet, and all were treated by X-rays, so that while there was no outward sign that they had been marked there would, according to the testimony of the Company, appear upon them when they were developed a design of the Company's trademark.

Carrying with him this doctored packet, and accompanied by a friend, Mr. Seymour, also a conjurer, Mr. Price kept an appointment which Mr. Hope had given him at the British College of Psychic Science, London, on February 24th, 1922. The mediums were quite unsuspicious of any trap, nor did they hear anything of the matter till four months later.

Mr. Price says: "I made myself very pleasant, said how sorry I was that they had been ill with influenza, and asked after the Crewe Circle, saying that my people were natives of Shropshire." A private detective must, of course, use deception, but when Mr. Price at a later stage proceeded to ask that "Onward, Christian soldiers!" be the hymn sung, and suggesting that the extra finally shown was that of his own mother, he really does seem to be wallowing in it to an unnecessary degree. After all, the matter was one of business; he had paid for his sitting, he would surely get it, and no elaborate deception was needed.

After the usual ceremonies Mr. Price and Mr. Hope went into the dark room, where the package was opened and the two top plates put into the carrier. Hope then took up the carrier, asking Price to wrap up the remaining plates, and it was at this moment that Price "saw him . . . put the dark slide to his left breast-pocket, and take it out again (another one?) without any 'talking' or knocking." I copy this sentence as printed, and it is curious to find the S.P.R., which is continually claiming from others the utmost exactness of statement, passing one which is so involved and unintelligible. However, it is certain that Mr. Price means that Hope at that moment changed the carriers, though he does not even tell us where the second carrier went to. Mr. Price had endeavoured to mark with some pricking instrument of his thumb the original carrier, but carriers are often of very hard wood, and he could not, one would think, have verified such a result, therefore the fact that no marks of pricks were found upon the carrier cannot be regarded very seriously. It is an instructive fact that the S.P.R receives all these very loose tests without question or comment, while when the evidence is the other way, as in the case of Major Spencer, they are ready with the most extraordinary explanations rather than admit a positive result.

The couple then emerged from the dark room—I am omitting unessential and wearying details—and the photographs were duly taken with no exact record of the time of exposure, though Mr. Price roughly placed it at from eighteen to nineteen seconds. The point was really of great, and might have been, of vital importance. When the plates were developed one was normal of Price alone, and the other had a female extra looking over Price's shoulder. This female face has the psychic arch and bears every sign to my eye, and to that of every spiritualist whom I have heard discuss it, of being true to type and a real Hope extra.

Mr. Price complimented the medium upon his success, carried off the plates, and then set himself to dictate an article which was duly printed in the "Proceedings" of the S.P.R. to show that the whole business was a swindle, that the plates had been changed, and that the extra had been on a plate which Hope had foisted upon Price by the device of changing the carriers in the dark room.

The points upon which Price relied in his charge may be taken in their order. They were:

1. That on the plate with the extra the X-ray marks of the Imperial Company were not present.

Experiments were at once undertaken by several investigators, including Dr. Cushman, of Washington, and Mr. Hewat McKenzie. They showed that with long exposures, such as Hope gave, the X-ray marks vanish, so that this test, as was admitted by the Imperial Company, ceases to be valid.

2. That he made marks upon the carrier, which were not found upon the carrier actually used.

These marks seem to have been mere pricks, and there is no independent evidence as to their existence.

3. That he saw Hope make a suspicious gesture in the dark room.

This would be more convincing if any indication could be given as to what became of the discarded carrier. In cross-examination Mr. Price weakened on the point.

4. That the glass of which the plates were made and on which the photos appeared, was different in colour and thickness from the glass of the Imperial plates brought by Mr. Price for the experiment.

This statement holds good. The plates have been examined and compared, and those who desired to guard the interests of Mr. Hope (or rather of truth) agreed that this contention was right, and that there had actually been a substitution of plates at some time by somebody. There we are all on common ground. How then, and why, were the plates changed?

Many who were convinced by experience of Hope's powers and of his essential honesty, and who were aware of the bitter antagonism which exists against him, as against all psychic phenomena, in certain circles of conjurers and of sceptical researchers, and of indiscreet expressions before the experiment, were of opinion that the whole transaction was an organised conspiracy to discredit the medium. The packet of plates had been for several weeks before the experiment in the possession of the officials of the S.P.R., and was accessible to clever-fingered people who were hostile to Hope's claims, and who had frequently averred that the opening of sealed packets was an easy process. There were other arguments which I will not state lest I should seem to be endorsing them. Let me say, at once, that I believe Messrs. Dingwall, Price and Seymour to be honourable gentlemen, however much I differ from their point of view, and that I will not advance any hypothesis which is not consistent with that position.*

At the same time, I would point out that all their difficulties, which have increased with fuller knowledge, are due to their own tortuous and indirect way of approaching the question. Suppose that instead of all this juggling of X-ray marks Mr. Price had simply initialled his plate the moment he took it from the packet as I and many other experimenters have done, surely if he had afterwards received an extra upon that initialled plate the test would have been complete, so far as substitution is concerned. If he had not done so, I am sure that Hope would have given him a second appointment, and he could have gone on until he had either succeeded or until he had proved that with an initialled plate Hope was helpless. Had this been done much trouble would have been saved, and the result been equally clear.

* I let these words stand as written, but further information, which only came later to my knowledge, has, as the text will show, caused me to take a less entirely charitable view.—A.C.D.

Or, again, when he was, as he says, morally sure that Hope had changed the carrier, suppose that instead of complimenting Hope upon results and suggesting that the image was that of his mother, he had said, "You will excuse me, Mr. Hope, but I must really examine you and your dark room, for I think I can find a marked carrier which you have concealed while you substituted your own." A refusal from Hope would have really been a confession. But, all through, a tortuous course was preferred.

I have nothing against Mr. Price's honour, but a very great deal against his methods, winding up with his sixpenny attack upon Hope, when the matter, as events have proved, was very far from being settled.

This pamphlet would certainly convey to the public the idea that Mr. Price looked upon psychic photography in general as the greatest humbug in the world, whereas since then he has signed a document which ends with the words:

"We are convinced that the test with Hope on February 24th does not rule out the possibility that Hope has produced supernormal pictures, or that he is able to produce 'extras' by other than normal means."

Had he been wise enough to adopt this humbler tone in the first instance we could all discuss the question now in a more placid frame of mind.

But irritability must not make us unjust, and we have to face the question how came the plates to be changed? The only honest answer is that we do not know, but that the evidence taken on its face value at this stage was against Hope, in spite of his long record of honesty.

FIG. 8.—The Rev. C. L. Tweedale and his wife with psychic likeness of Mrs. Tweedale's father. (*See* p. 34.)

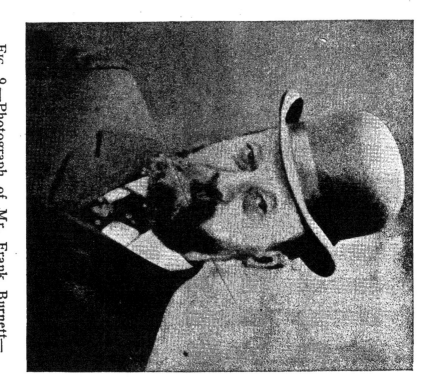

FIG. 9.—Photograph of Mr. Frank Burnett—Mrs. Tweedale's father—who died in 1913. Compare with Fig. 8, showing psychic likeness

Fig. 11.—Photograph of Mr. and Mrs. H. East, with psychic likeness of their son obtained on a surprise visit to Crewe. Normal photograph re-

Fig. 10.—Photograph of Mrs. Buxton of the Crewe Circle with her daughter. Psychic likeness of Mrs. Buxton's father unlike any other picture in existence.

AN EXAMINATION OF MR. HOPE

Mr. Barlow has put forward the plea that Hope was in an abnormal mental condition at such times, and was to that extent irresponsible. I fear I cannot accept this, for such substitution must be thought out beforehand, an image must be prepared, and the whole transaction is not an act of impulse but a deliberate plan.

There has, however, been a most singular sequel to the case which causes an extraordinary complication, and when closely examined seems to me to turn Hope from the defendant into the accuser. The S.P.R. claims that after this experiment one of the two marked plates had been returned to them, but in so secret a fashion that it could not be explained who had brought it or how it had been obtained. This was apparently a point against Hope, the charge inferred, though not stated, being that he had left this plate about, after abstracting it from the carrier, and that some enemy had recognised it and brought it to clinch the case against him. So secret were the proceedings of the Society that though I am one of the oldest members of that body I was refused leave to see this mysterious plate. Eventually, however, some of our people did see it, and then an extraordinary state of things revealed itself. First of all the plate was undoubtedly one of the original set supplied by the Imperial Dry Plate Company. Secondly, it was a virgin unexposed plate, so that it is impossible that anyone at Hope's end could have picked it out from any other plates, since the marks were invisible. Third, and most wonderful, it actually, on being developed, had an image upon it, which may or may not have been a psychic extra. This plate was sent on March 3rd, a week after the experiment and three

[47]

days after Hope and Mrs. Buxton, who knew nothing yet of Price's trap, had returned home to Crewe. It was in a double wrapper, with a request upon the inside cover that it be developed. The wrapper was formed of Psychic College literature, and it bore the Notting Hill postmark.

Now consider the situation thus created. Since the plate had not been developed it is clear that neither Hope nor anyone at the College could possibly have known that it was a marked plate, for there was no publication of the alleged exposure until more than four months after. Who was there in the whole world who did know that this was a marked plate and one in which the S.P.R. might be expected to take a special interest? Clearly the experimenters of the S.P.R. and their confidants—no one else. But if the marked plate had been abstracted by Hope in the dark room and mixed up there with other plates, how could any friend or emissary of the S.P.R. have picked it out as being the plate that was marked? It could not have been done. Therefore the conclusion seems to be irresistible that this plate was abstracted from the packet *before* the experiment by someone who knew exactly what it was. If this be so, Hope is the victim of a conspiracy and he is a much ill-used man. I see no possible alternative to this conclusion.

Let us see if we can build up any sort of theory which would cover all the known facts. Any such theory is bound to be improbable, but the improbable is better than the impossible, and it is quite impossible that Hope could have known that a plate was secretly marked when it had not been exposed or developed.

AN EXAMINATION OF MR. HOPE

We have to remember that the knot of conspirators (some consciously so, and some not) are in close touch with a group of conjurers. These gentlemen have announced that there is no packet which cannot be opened and no seal which cannot be tampered with undetected. For twenty-four days after Mr. Price takes his packet of marked plates to the headquarters of the S.P.R. it was locked up not in a safe but in an ordinary drawer, which may or may not have been locked, but could presumably be easily opened. My belief is that during that long period the packet was actually opened and the top plates taken out. Upon one of these top plates a faked photograph was thrown from one of those small projectors which produce just such an effect as is shown on the returned plate. The idea may have been that Hope would claim this effect as his own and that he would then be confounded by the announcement that it was there all the time. That was the first stage. The second stage was that either the original conspirator relented or someone else who was in his confidence thought it was too bad, so the packet was again tampered with, the marked and faked plate taken out and a plain one substituted. The packet was then taken to Hope as described. Mr. Hope then got a perfectly honest psychic effect upon the unmarked plate. Meanwhile the abstracter, whoever he may have been, had the original faked plate in his possession, and out of a spirit of pure mischief—for I can imagine no other reason—he wrapped it in a sheet of the College syllabus, which can easily be obtained, and returned it to the S.P.R., to whom it originally belonged. Wherever it came from it is clear that it did not come from the

College, for when a man does a thing secretly and anonymously he does not enclose literature which will lead to his detection.

It is possible that this thing may originally have been conceived as a sort of practical joke upon Hope and upon spiritualists generally, but that some who were not in the joke have pushed the matter further than was originally intended. Whom can we blame? I am in the position of never having personally met any of the three protagonists, Price, Dingwall or Seymour, so that my view of them is impartial. Mr. Price is popular among the spiritualists who know him, and all agree that he would be unlikely to lend himself to any deception. Mr. Dingwall was possessed by an extreme prejudice against Mr. Hope, and yet I cannot conceive him as gratifying that prejudice by such a trick. He cannot, however, be acquitted of having aided and abetted in issuing the libellous pamphlet against Hope before all the facts were known, and before Hope's friends could examine any of them. It was an unworthy thing to do, and Messrs. Price and Dingwall must share the responsibility. It is a curious fact which should be recorded that, although the experiment was on February 24th, and though the report of the alleged exposure was not issued till the end of May, we find Mr. Dingwall applying for a sitting with Hope early in May, and writing, when Hope refused to give him one: "As I understand from your letters that you still refuse to have sittings with the only scientific body in Great Britain investigating this subject, I shall be obliged in my coming report on psychic photography to publish certain facts which may not be of advantage to yourself." That letter was on May 2nd. Apparently, therefore, the publication of the "exposure" depended upon whether Mr. Dingwall was piqued or was humoured. If he were sure that the exposure was a genuine one this is a very singular attitude to assume.

There remains Mr. James Seymour, the amateur conjurer, who has been concerned in several so-called exposures. It would be unjust to assert that it was he who carried out this deception, for when a packet is left for twenty-four days in a drawer many people may have had access to it, and none of the three experimenters may have known the facts. This, I think, is very probable. At the same time, as Mr. Seymour has been very searching in his inquiries about mediums, he will not take it amiss if I ask him what he meant when in his evidence ("Cold Light," etc., p. 7) he says: "They" (*i.e.*, Hope and Mrs. Buxton) "were thoroughly taken in by the packet and were not suspicious of it." How could they possibly be suspicious of a packet which had never been opened? On the other hand, if the speaker knew that the packet had been tampered with, it would be a most natural remark to make. The words may be innocent, but they demand a clear explanation, and so does the fact that an extra was found upon a marked plate which obviously had never been in Hope's dark room at all.

So secretive and tortuous have been the methods of the agents of the S.P.R that each fresh piece of evidence has to be wrung from them, and they seem to have no conception of the fact that a man who is accused has a right to know all the facts concerning the accusation. Even now, nine months after the event, constant pressure has to be put upon them in order to get at the truth. Only at this last moment has a new and strange fact been admitted. It is that when the mysterious marked plate was returned it was not alone, but that three other plates, not belonging to the marked series, were with it, *each* of them adorned with psychic photographs. These photographs in no way resembled the results of Hope or of Mrs. Deane, nor were they like the one upon the marked plate. I should be interested to know whether Mr. Marriott was ever in the counsels of the conspirators, for there is something in this incident which rather recalls that gentlemen's powers and also his somewhat impish sense of humour.

Even now—I write nearly nine months after the original investigation—we have no assurance that this secret of the S.P.R. has been fully divulged or that they have been frank with the public. It is possible that they have received other anonymous communications which bear upon the case. The first one was within a week of the investigation, and if divulged at the time it might have been possible to find the source. After such a lapse of time it is far more difficult. As I have shown, these new facts place the Society in a very invidious position and that may be the cause of their hesitations and concealments, but they have to remember that they have made a wanton attack upon a man's honour, and that their own *amour propre* is a small thing compared to the admission of the injustice they have done. They should now come forward honestly, admit the blunders they have committed, apologise to Hope, and remove any slur which they have cast upon one of the most important and consistent psychic

manifestations ever known in the history of the move-
ment. In all attempted explanations let them bear in
mind the central fact that no one but themselves and
their associates knew that there was a marked plate in
existence until several months after the experiment and
after one had been returned to them.

Among those who examined the evidence at that
time available was Dr. Allerton Cushman, for whose
independence of mind and strong common sense I have
a great respect. Having signed the document in which
he admitted that there had been substitution of plates,
he added the following impressive note:

"My signature appended to the above statement
sets forth that investigation of all the facts available
up to date shows that the plate containing the psychic
extra in the Price test sitting with Hope did not
match up with the other plates marked by the Imperial Dry Plate Company. The only possible inference is that the plate in question was substituted by
someone at some time either deliberately or acci-
dentally. I do not commit myself as to the authorship of the substitution. After careful experimenta-
tion I do not consider the system of X-ray marking
adopted by Mr. Price to be infallible, but quite the
reverse, as the markings quite disappear on long exposures and over-development. I am also unim-
pressed and unconvinced by Mr. Price's method of
marking the plate-holder. I have had in all five
sittings with Hope and four with Mrs. Deane. Of
these nine sittings, seven were conducted under test
conditions in which Dr. H. Carrington and other witnesses participated. I have obtained psychic extras
from both mediums on plates marked by X-ray by
the Imperial Dry Plate Company, and boxed and
sealed by them, and also on plates purchased by Dr.

Carrington just previous to one of the Hope sitting
all of which were marked by us with every preca
tion. I am convinced that there was no substituti
possible in at least five of the seven test sittings.
consider that the mediums possess genuine psy
power, and are capable of obtaining marvellc
genuine results. . . . The more I investigate
subject the more convinced I am that the marvell
evidential case of spirit photography obtained by
through Mrs. Deane in July, 1921, was genuine ai
true.

        "Yours faithfully,
      "ALLERTON F. CUSHMAN."

CHAPTER V

It might well be urged, "Why should Hope go into the dark room at all? Why should he not allow the sitter to charge his carrier by himself and so remove all possibility of transposition?" It is natural that Hope should show the stranger where the various conveniences of the dark room are, but apart from this there is the reason that Hope in the course of his career has had all sorts of tricks played upon him by dishonest investigators, and that he has to protect himself, so far as he can, against doctored plates or plates with extras already prepared which will be ascribed to him and made the ground for charges. I have heard him tell such instances. When he knows his sitter he has no objection at all to leaving him alone in the dark room.

In 1919 the Society which I have already referred to as the S.S.S.P. presented Hope with a new camera. Mr. Barlow, Mr. Pearse and Mr. Walker—all experienced photographers—were the three delegates who conveyed it to Crewe. On this occasion photographs were taken with the new carriers and camera, *Mr. Barlow loading the carrier with his own plate alone in the dark room.* In developing, all three delegates went into the dark room, but Hope did not accompany them. Three out of four slides showed no supernormal result, but the forth showed three faces, one clearly recognised.

"We were carefully watching Mr. Hope all the time and are absolutely sure that there was no trickery." The document, which contains a detailed account of these facts, is signed by all three observers. Could any case be more satisfactory and more final?

I have said that professional photographers were among the sitters. I would instance as a good example Mr. A. R. Gibson, of Nottingham, who testifies that he took every possible precaution against deceit, and that none the less he received an excellent likeness of his dead son which does not correspond to any existing photograph and is recognised by all who knew the lad.

There is one final case to which I would particularly desire to draw attention because it is exactly parallel to that of Mr. Price, but had a diametrically opposite result. The inquirer, too, has the advantage of being absolutely impartial, which cannot be said of the two conjurers nor of Mr. Dingwall, who was behind them —and even with every intention to be honest, a strong bias can distort the results. The case to which I refer is that of Mrs. St. Clair Stobart, of 7, Turners Wood, Hampstead Garden Suburb, who sat to Mr. Hope in March, 1921. Before the sitting Mrs. Stobart's plates were marked with a secret mark, which she herself did not know, by the Kodak Company. The result is told in full in *Psychic Science* for October of this year. Briefly, after every conceivable precaution by Mrs. Stobart and her husband, two extras were got in four attempts, one a head only and the other a full-length figure of a woman, clothed in the usual filmy drapery. "Mr. Hope never handled the plates at all." Mrs. Stobart concludes: "I took the negatives to the Kodak

Company—to the manager and chief assistant. 'Are these the plates you marked? Can you see the marks?' I asked. 'Oh yes,' they replied. 'Look, here they are— a tiny circle enclosing a cross.' And for the first time I saw the marks which they had put. The Kodak Company allow me to say that their affirmation as to this can be used freely."

Now surely this is very important. There seems no loophole for error, and it entirely reverses the results of the S.P.R. Why should more credit be given to one than the other? Of the two, Mrs. Stobart's is undoubtedly the more scientific, for we have no story of plates being left about for twenty-four days before an experiment, and, as I have pointed out, there is no possible bias. Taken with all the other examples which I have given, and with those given later by Mr. Barlow, I claim that no reasonable man can doubt that Hope's hands are clean. It is the S.P.R. clique with their tortuous methods, and with their mystery plate unexplained, who can most reasonably be accused of a want of frank, straightforward dealing. It is sad to think that a society which has done good work in the past, and which has been made famous by the labours of great spiritualists like Myers and Hodgson, Barrett and Crookes, should be mixed up at all with so ugly a business handled in so questionable a way.

Before bringing to an end this short sketch of the work of the Crewe Circle, I would beg the reader to consider the positive cases which I have laid before him and to remember that in order to establish the intervention of external, intelligent forces—which is our sole and only aim—we have only to make *one* case good.

One positive case outweighs all the negative ones which the industry of the most energetic "exposer" could collect. Our enemies take the perverse course of dwelling entirely upon negative results, a line of reasoning which would have killed any science in the world. They know, as a matter of fact, very little about the subject, for starting, as they do, with the presumption that it is a palpable fraud, they do not devote to it the time and the close study which it calls for.

There is only one body in this country which can claim any authority, and that is the S.S.S.P., or Society for the Study of Supernormal Pictures, of which Dr. Abraham Wallace is President, while I share with Mr. Mitchell and Mr. Blackwell the honour of being vice-president. We number among our members Miss Scatcherd, whose experience is probably unique, Mr. Coates, who has written two excellent books upon the subject, Colonel Baddeley, Major Spencer, whose experiments have extended over many years, Colonel Johnson, a pioneer investigator, professional and expert photographers, and others of all shades of opinions, save that all, so far as I know, are convinced by actual experience of the reality of the phenomenon. Of its methods and curious, almost inconceivable and most freakish manifestations we have collected a mass of material and have even cleared a few permanent pathways among the jungle.

It is to this society, and not to the S.P.R. as at present conducted, that the world may look for accurate information upon this subject. It would not be reasonable for me to go at any length here into the results obtained. I would only say that so far as my own conclusions go, basing my studies upon the photographers of the past as well as the present, I think that the evidence is strong that there is on the other side an intelligent control for each photographic medium, whose powers are great but by no means unlimited and who endeavours to give us convincing results each in his own characteristic way. These results are sometimes obtained by actual materialisations, sometimes by precipitations of pictures apart from exposure, sometimes, as I believe, by the superposition of screens which have the psychic face already upon them, and which give marks as of a double exposure. Among the powers of the control is to build up a simulacrum which may be the image of someone who is still alive, or he may produce upon the plate facsimiles of pictures and portraits which do at present exist, but which are entirely beyond the normal reach of the medium. All these and other equally strange points I could illustrate by many examples, but their mere recital will show how many snares lie before the explorer, and how many things might seem to be fraudulent when they are really the doing not of the medium but of the control.

Any further expansion of this fascinating subject would be out of place on my part, since I am by no means one of the authorities, and can only claim that I study and assimilate the results of others, to which, of course, I add my own personal experience. I have, however, asked Mr. Barlow, the Honorary Secretary of this Society, whose experience is so extensive as to be almost unrivalled, to add a short essay upon the subject, with an account of some of the cases which bear upon the matter.

CHAPTER VI

THE ATTACK ON MRS. DEANE AND MR. VEARNCOMBE

I TOOK up my pen for the purpose of considering the case of the Crewe Circle and urging the folly of discarding the work of seventeen years on the score of a single case. I cannot, however, end my task without saying a few words as to the attack upon Mrs. Deane and Mr. Vearncombe, two other photographic mediums. This attack hardly deserves attention as it was anonymous, but it was brought out under the auspices of the Magic Circle, a society of conjurers who have been interesting themselves in matters psychic. As the two attacks were issued almost simultaneously they seem to have had some common inspiration, and to have formed a general assault upon the whole position of psychic photography. The same individual, Mr. Seymour, the amateur conjurer, actually took part, I understand, in both transactions.

Mrs. Deane, the person attacked, is a somewhat pathetic and forlorn figure among all these clever tricksters. She is a little, elderly charwoman, a humble white mouse of a person, with her sad face, her frayed gloves, and her little handbag which excites the worst suspicions in the minds of her critics. Her powers were discovered in the first instance quite by chance. When she first pursued the subject her circumstances were such that her only dark room was under the kitchen table with clothes pinned round it. None the less, she produced some remarkable pictures under these conditions, one of which fell into my hands, and I at once concluded that she had real powers. The portrait was of a young man in life, with a female spirit face behind him. This might well have been faked. Something seemed to be emerging from the young man's head, however, and on observing this object with a lens I distinguished that it was a small but correct representation of the Assyrian fish-god, Dagon, wearing the peculiar hat with which that deity is always associated. This was so entirely the kind of freakish result which I expect from spirit photography, and was so removed from the normal powers of a charwoman, that I provisionally accepted her in my mind as a true medium, a position from which I have never been compelled to budge. I still retain this photograph, but the little head is too small for satisfactory reproduction.

Mrs. Deane (or Mrs. Deane's control) has one embarrassing habit which I believe to be unnecessary, and which makes it very difficult to convince the sceptic, or, indeed, to prevent him from writing her down as an obvious fraud. Far from insisting that you bring your own plates, as Hope does, she likes them to be sent to her in advance, and she does what she calls "magnetising" them, by keeping them near her for some days. This is so suspicious that it can hardly be defended, but here, again, there is an element of fanatical obedience. My own personal belief is that her results are perfectly honest, that they are actually formed in the shape of psychographs during the days before the sitting, and that if her plates were examined before they were exposed to light, the pictures would be found already on them. This, of course, would very naturally be taken as clear proof of fraud by the superficial investigator, ignorant of the strange possibilities of psychic photography, but I believe myself that the psychic effect is a perfectly genuine one, but that the extra will very probably bear no relevancy to the sitter. I am speaking now of her general routine, for how can I guarantee every particular case or judge what a medium may do when dealing with so evanescent and elusive a thing as psychic power? When they have it they use it—when it fails them the human element may come in.

I have had one sitting with Mrs. Deane in which six plates were exposed. In four of them there were abnormal results. One of these was a female face smiling from an ectoplasmic cloud. What does Mrs. Deane know of ectoplasmic clouds? One such is visible in the specimen of her work which is shown in Figure 30. Exactly similar are some of the clouds which appear in Hope's work. Such appearances do not aid deception. Why, then, should they appear if it is not that it is part of a psychic process?

Mrs. Deane gave me the choice of two packets of plates upon this occasion, and I admit that the effects may very well have been on the plates before the exposure. None the less, they were probably quite genuine as supernormal pictures. Such a statement may raise a smile from Mr. MacCabe or from Mr. Paternoster in *Truth*, but I have the advantage over them in the fact that I have had practical experience of the matter at issue.

But I am bound to give my reasons for such a state-

FIG. 12.—Photograph of Mr. Wm. Jeffrey and his daughter, showing ectoplasmic bag. (*See* p. 37.)

FIG. 13.—Photograph taken immediately after that shown by Fig. 12. Position of sitters is unchanged, but the ectoplasmic veiling now contains an excellent likeness (slightly distorted) of Mr. Jeffrey's de-ceased wife.

Fig. 15.—A normal photograph of Agnes. Cushman for comparison with Fig. 14.

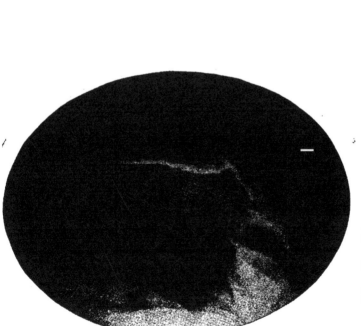

Fig. 14.—Psychic likeness of Agnes, daughter of Dr. Allerton Cushman. A life-like picture obtained by Dr. Cushman through a surprise visit paid to Mrs. Dean. (*See* p. 63.)

ment, or I might well be branded as credulous. My reasons are that I am convinced that this magnetising process is perfectly unnecessary and Mrs. Deane, within my knowledge, obtains her best results when there has been no possibility of knowing who her sitter will be. The very finest result which I know of in psychic photography was that obtained by Dr. Cushman with Mrs. Deane. Dr. Cushman, a distinguished scientific man of America, had suffered the loss of his daughter Agnes some months before. He went to the Psychic College without an appointment or an introduction. When he arrived he found Mrs. Deane in the act of leaving. He persuaded her to give a sitting, and then and there he obtained a photograph of his "dead" daughter which is, he declares, unlike any existing one, and is more vital and characteristic than any taken in life. When I was in the States I showed this picture on the screen as in Figure 14, and there was abundant testimony from those who knew Agnes that it was a life-like picture.

I would refer this case to the anonymous writers of the Magic Circle, who has done all they could to worry this poor woman and to destroy her powers, and I would ask them how that little bag of tricks which exists only in their own imagination could have affected such a result as that. It will be noted in the already quoted opinion of Dr. Cushman that since this scandal Mrs. Deane has been severely tested by him and others, and that they have been able under the Doctor's own conditions to get psychic results.

Another excellent case of Mrs. Deane's power is that which forms the subject of Figure 30. The extra in the ectoplasmic cloud is Mr. Barlow, senior, the father of

[63]

the Secretary of the S.S.S.P. Beside him is a picture
of how he looked twelve years before his death. No
one can deny that it is the same man with the years
added on. Mrs. Deane never knew Mr. Barlow's father
in life. How, then, was this result obtained? These
are the cases which the Magic Circle report avoids,
while it talks much of any negative results which it can
collect or imagine. I hope that this short account may
do something towards helping a woman whom I believe to be a true psychic, and who has suffered severely
for the faith that is in her, having actually, I understand, endured the excommunication of her church because she has used the powers which God has given
her. I have a recollection that Joan of Arc endured
the same fate for the reason *"le plus il change, le plus
il reste le même."*

It only remains for me now, before giving place to
others, to say a word about Mr. Vearncombe, the
psychic photographer of Bridgwater. Mr. Vearncombe
was a normal, professional photographer, but he found,
as Mumler did, that inexplicable extras intruded upon
and spoilt both his plates and his business. He then
began to study this new power, which he seemed to possess, and to develop it for commercial use. Mrs. Hum-
phreys, a member of the S.S.S.P. and a student of
psychic affairs, lived in the same town and submitted
him to certain tests which convinced her and others of
his *bona fides,* though I cannot repeat too often that no
blank cheque of honesty can ever be given to any man.

My own experience of Mr. Vearncombe and my
knowledge of his work are far less than in the cases of
Mr. Hope and Mrs. Deane, so that I can only say that

[64]

MRS. DEANE AND MR. VEARNCOMBE

I believe he produces genuine results, whereas in the other two cases I can say that I *know* they produce genuine results.

I have had two experiments with Vearncombe, but did not impose any test conditions in either case. I simply sent a closed envelope containing a letter and asked him to photograph it in the hope that some extra might appear which I could associate with the sender of the letter. In both cases a large number, six or seven, well-marked faces developed round the letter, but none which bore any message to me. Others, however, have been more fortunate in their experience and have assured me that they have received true pictures of the dead in that fashion. There is no ectoplasmic cloud or psychic arch, but the faces are as clear-cut as if they were stamped with a die.

I am in some degree responsible for Vearncombe's troubles, as I mentioned his name as being one who might repay investigation upon the occasion when I gave evidence before a committee of these conjuring gentlemen. They seem to have made up a sealed packet to Mr. Vearncombe with instructions to get what he could. Upon its return they declared that the packet, which had furnished a psychic result, had been tampered with. No independent proof whatever was offered in support of this assertion, and Mr. Fred Barlow, who had obtained results from Mr. Vearncombe, where he was sure that the packets had *not* been tampered with, was sufficiently interested to hunt up the name of the sender and some details of the case from the Vearncombe end, rather than from that of the "exposers." Fortunately Vearncombe had preserved the letters, and

[65]

THE CASE FOR SPIRIT PHOTOGRAPHY

it was then found that the sender, when the packet and the psychic result had been returned, had at once written to Vearncombe to acknowledge receipt, adding the two statements:

(1) That one of the faces strongly recalled "an old true friend who had not been heard of for many years," and
(2) That the packet had been returned intact.

Thus the Magic Circle had clearly fallen into the pit that it had digged, and its agent is convicted either of being a senseless liar without any cause, or else of having completely endorsed the result which the Circle afterwards pretended was a failure. It was one of those numerous instances when it is not the medium but the investigators who should really be exposed. My experience is that this is the case far more frequently than the public can realise, and that it is amazing how men of honour can turn and twist the facts when they deal with this subject. A well-known "exposer" assured a friend of mine that he would think nothing of putting muslin in a medium's pocket at a séance, if he was sure that he could thereby secure a conviction.

I have seen a letter from Mr. Marriott, who is also busy in showing up "frauds," in which, writing to Mr. Hope, he offered to teach him to make more artistic spirit-photographs, charging thirty guineas if the lessons were in London and forty if at Crewe. I am quite prepared to anticipate Mr. Marriott's explanation that this was a trap, but it is an example of the tortuous, deceptive methods against which our mediums have to contend.

MRS. DEANE AND MR. VEARNCOMBE

I understand that Mr. Vearncombe is so disgusted with the whole episode that he declares he will demonstrate his powers no longer, save to private friends. We can but hope that he will not allow ignorant or dishonest anonymous criticism to influence him to this extent. If all of us who endure annoyance, and even insult, were to desert the spiritualist cause in order to save our private feelings, we could hardly expect the truth to prevail.

Let me conclude by saying that I speak from a far larger experience than the representatives of the S.P.R. or of the Magic Circle, and that, leaving out Mr. Vearncombe, who needs no defence in the face of the admission quoted above, I have no doubt whatever of the true psychic powers of Mrs. Deane and of Mr. Hope, though I cannot pronounce upon every single case at which I was not present and when I have had no opportunity of examining the complete evidence. I fear that the most permanent result of this episode will be that the spiritualists will very reasonably refuse the present régime of the Research Society all access to their mediums, since experience has shown that they may, without a chance of self-defence, be attacked in consequence in a cheap, popular pamphlet before even the case has been examined by any impartial authority.

POSTSCRIPT

At the last moment before this booklet goes to press, I am able to insert the fact that Hope's complete innocence has now been clearly established, and he stands before the world as a man who has been very cruelly maligned, and the victim of a plot which has been quite extraordinary in its ramifications. It was at last found possible to get the cover in which the original packet of plates was wrapped, and on it were found unmistakable signs that it had been tampered with and opened. Thus the deductions made in the text from the evidence already to hand have been absolutely justified, and it is clear that the marked plates were abstracted before the packet reached the Psychic College and two ordinary plates substituted, upon one of which Hope produced an "extra." The conclusion was reached by the acumen and patience of Mr. Hewat McKenzie, but his results were examined and endorsed unanimously by a strong committee, which included, besides myself, Mr. and Mrs. McKenzie, General Carter, Colonel Baddeley, Mr. Stanley de Brath, Mrs. Stobart, Miss V. R. Scatcherd, Mrs. de Crespigny, Mr. H. C. Scofield and Mr. F. Bligh Bond. It now only remains to find out who is the culprit who has played this cunning trick, and it is not difficult to say that the hand which returned the marked plate through the post is the same hand as that which took it out of the packet. A reward has already been offered for the identification of the person concerned. In the meantime it would be unfair to blame the agents of the S.P.R., who may, while trying to trick Hope, have been themselves tricked. Nothing, however, can excuse them from the charge of culpable negligence in failing to examine the wrappers which so clearly tell the story, and which have been kept so long in their possession. As the matter stands, five persons stand as defendants: Mr. Harry Price, Mr. Moger, Mr. James Seymour, Miss Newton, Secretary of the S.P.R., and Mr. Dingwall, Research Officer of that body. If there is someone else in the background who has tricked them, then it is for them to find out who it is. Their negligence has been such that it is difficult to say what atonement can meet it, and it throws a very lurid light upon some of the so-called "exposures" of the past. As one of the oldest members of the S.P.R., I feel that the honour of that body will not be cleared until they have appointed an impartial committee to consider these facts and to determine what steps should be taken.

ARTHUR CONAN DOYLE.

November 14th, 1922.

CHAPTER VII

THE GENESIS AND HISTORY OF THE CREWE CIRCLE

BY F. R. SCATCHERD

Member of the Society for Psychical Research,
Co-Editor of the *Asiatic Review*

(Miss Felicia Scatcherd, who has been one of the true psychic researchers and pioneers of knowledge in this country, has contributed the following information which she gained during her close association with the Crewe Circle at and after the time of its formation.)

QUESTIONED about himself, Mr. Hope said that he was christened "Billy Hope," and was born at or near Manchester. His first memory is of having scarlet fever when he was four years old. During the fever he used to see all sorts of faces peering at him through the doorway, and became so frightened that he screamed for his father to come and send them away. Now that he knows about clairvoyance, he thinks otherwise of those visions. He lost his mother when he was nine, and remembers little about her. It is a curious fact, as he observed: "I have wished for her picture hundreds of times, and sat for it many a while, and have never yet got it. These things beat me."

When asked did he grieve much for his mother's death, he replied that he was brought up in a religious family, his father being a local preacher. Later on Mr. Hope, Senior, lost all his worldly possessions.

"My father was wealthy according to my ideas,"

[70]

said Mr. Hope. "He had two farms, but late in life lost his money."

Mr. Hope was well cared for by his mother as long as he had her, and afterwards by his step-mother.

"She was a good woman: and I had an aunt of a religious frame of mind who also kept an eye on me."

"You must have been a very good little boy," I said.

"Oh dear, no! I was much the same as the other lads. I played plenty of truant, and once joined a party of seven and ran the schoolmaster round the room. We had agreed beforehand what we would do if he began a-thrashing of us. But don't put that in, Miss Scatcherd!"

Spirit photography first interested him when he was working at a bleach and dye-works near Pendleton. Being an amateur photographer, he and a comrade agreed to photograph each other one Saturday afternoon. Mr. Hope exposed a plate on his friend and developed it, when they saw a woman standing beside him. The brick wall showed through the figure, there being no background. The sitter, a Roman Catholic, was frightened, and asked how the woman had got on the plate, and did Mr. Hope know her. When Mr. Hope replied that he did not know the lady nor how she got there, *the man said it was his sister who had been dead for many years.*

Neither knew anything of spiritualism, so they took it to the works on Monday and showed it to their foreman, who happened also to be an amateur photographer, and was "lost in wonder" over it. But there was a fellow worker, a spiritualist, who said it was a spirit photo. The foreman arranged that the experiment

[71]

should be repeated with the same camera the following Saturday, when not only the identical woman appeared again but with her, her little dead baby.

"I thought this very strange," said Mr. Hope; "it made me more interested in spirit photography, and I have been dabbling at it ever since. I felt sorry for my mate, he was so scared. When he saw the second result, I thought he would have pegged out" (died of fright).

The Circle used to destroy all negatives. The members did not want anyone to know about their spirit photography, as many people did not want to do business with them, saying it was all the devil's work. Till the advent of Archdeacon Colley on the scene not a single negative was kept. After a print was taken the negative was destroyed.

Mr. and Mrs. Buxton met Mr. Hope some seventeen years ago at the Spiritualist Hall at Crewe, where Mr. Buxton was organist. After the service Mr. Hope asked Mr. Buxton if he could find one or two friends to form a circle to sit for spirit photography. This was done, and it was arranged to use the next Wednesday evening from eight to nine.

One of the circle of six was a non-spiritualist, but was converted when a picture of his father and mother was obtained. A strange thing is that when all were anxiously desiring a picture, a message appeared on the first plate exposed. This message promised a picture next time, and stated that it would be for the master of the house. The promise was kept several sittings later, when the picture of Mr. Buxton's mother and of Mrs. Buxton's sister came on the plate. Mr. Buxton was of the opinion that this was given to do away with the idea of thought photography. They were all thinking of a picture and never dreamed that such a thing as a written message would be given. They have been very persevering, having sat regularly ever since, each Wednesday from eight to nine, securing a picture on an average of one a month at the outset.

There have been many storms before which have broken over the Crewe Circle, but the cause of them has usually been the limited knowledge of the strange possibilities ol psychic photography on the part of the sitters and of the public. One of the most notorious of these so-called "exposures" (which really were exposures of the critics' ignorance) was in 1908, and arose out of Archdeacon Colley's first sitting. He had heard that the Crewe Circle were simple-looking folk, and this attracted him, so he broke his journey at Crewe and called upon Mr. and Mrs. Hope, who had just lost their eldest daughter. The Archdeacon apologised for having come at such a time, but Mr. Hope sent him on to Mr. and Mrs. Buxton, where he was shown the photos and asked to see the negatives. He was shocked when he heard that they had all been destroyed, and from that time kept all negatives he was able to get hold of. The Archdeacon brought his own camera, loaded at Stockton with his own diamond-marked plates. He kept the plates in his own possession and focussed the camera, *which he put up outside the house,* although it was raining. Mr. Hope merely pressed the bulb and Archdeacon Colley developed the plates with his own developer. When he held the picture to the light he exclaimed: "My father and my sainted mother!"

THE CASE FOR SPIRIT PHOTOGRAPHY

Mr. Hope was the first to notice the likeness between "Mrs. Colley" and a picture he had copied about two years ago, and cycled with it to Mr. Spencer, of Nantwich. Mrs. Spencer declared it to be her grandmother, and cried out, "Oh, if this had only come with us how pleased we should have been!"

Mr. Hope then wrote to Archdeacon Colley telling him it could not be his mother, as it had been recognised at Nantwich. The Archdeacon said it was madness to think a man did not know his own mother, and advertised in the Leamington paper, asking all who remembered his mother to meet him at the Rectory, when eighteen persons selected the photograph from several others and testified in writing that the picture was a portrait of the late Mrs. Colley, who had never been photographed.

The Crewe friends heard no more about the matter until the controversy in *Light* (February 14th, 1914, and subsequent numbers). The extraordinary ignorance, even of the spiritualistic public, on these matters, was revealed by the storm of indignation that burst upon the devoted heads of the Crewe Circle and their supporters. The testimony of such students and scholars as the late Mr. James W. Sharpe, M.A., of Bournemouth, an eminent mathematician and expert authority on all questions of psychical research, did little to allay the outburst. In vain it was pointed out that no fact was better vouched for than the reproduction by "spirit" photographers of well-known pictures and photographs, often true in every detail to the originals. The theory and fact of ideoplasticity were ridiculed just as they are ridiculed to-day by those who should keep themselves

[74]

up-to-date in physical science, if they wish to judge justly the yet more complex problems of psychical science.

The Society for Psychical Research was as unhelpful as the "man in the street," so far as its leading authorities were concerned.

To return to the beginning of things: it was on July 16th, 1909, when, in response to a telegram from Archdeacon Colley, I went to Leamington, where I first met the Rev. Prof. Henslow and two members of the Crewe Circle who were on a visit to the Archdeacon. A séance for spirit photography was held. It was disappointing in one sense. Prof. Henslow was told that he would find impressions on certain plates in a sealed packet on the table *which was not to be opened for a fortnight.*

I prepared to say good-bye, when Mr. Hope said he would like to do something for the visitor from London. "The friends say that if the lady can remain the night they will give her a test." I replied that the only test of interest to me was one that would convince my fellow-members of the Society for Psychical Research. The mediums insisted, but I refused to stay unless Prof. Henslow also remained and took charge of the proceedings.

"Sir, do stay!" pleaded Mr. Hope. "There are five of us—you, the Archdeacon, Mrs. Buxton, Miss Scatcherd and myself. You must buy five plates from your own photographer. Each plate must be put into a light-tight envelope and worn by the sitter, with the sensitised surface next to the person, until the séance. It will not take long to fetch the plates and bring them back to us. Thus we shall have an hour to wear them before the séance this evening. It is the only way to get them magnetised so as to have immediate results. You cån each develop your own plate to-night and then Miss Scatcherd will know whether the friends have kept their word."

Prof. Henslow good-naturedly agreed and drove off with the Archdeacon to purchase the plates. I remained with Mrs. Buxton and Mr. Hope. Within an hour the Archdeacon returned with four plates put up as directed. Professor Henslow had gone home to dinner wearing his plate in a wood slide contrived by Archdeacon Colley. Mrs. Buxton and I tucked ours inside our blouses and Mr. Hope placed his in that trouser-pocket which has aroused such evil suspicions in the minds of investigators. We remained together until Prof. Henslow joined us. It was full daylight We sat round the table when Mr. Hope asked:

"What do you want, Miss Scatcherd? A face? A message? What shall it be?"

"You forget my conditions; Prof. Henslow must decide. Let him choose," I replied.

Prof. Henslow said he did not care what came so' long as *the same thing appeared on all the plates.* It was a remark worthy of the speaker, conveying, as it did, a most crucial test, in view of the fact that he had never let his plate out of his own keeping. The usual séance was held.

Prof. Henslow developed his plate first. I developed mine under Archdeacon Colley's supervision, then Mrs. Buxton and Mr. Hope developed theirs.

The results are of interest. The Archdeacon did not wear a plate so as to leave "more power for the others."

Mr. Hope's plate was blurred. The tablet on Prof. Henslow's was identical in outline with Mrs. Buxton's and mine, both of which were sharp and clear, but Mrs. Buxton's was the best. Mrs. Buxton had been with me the whole time, and her six-months-old baby had never left her arms.

The message addressed to Prof. Henslow was appropriate, but the writing was so microscopically fine that we could not read it that night. Mr. Hope was very disappointed. "Never mind," he said, "when we get home we will ask the guides to give it us again!" He and Mrs. Buxton were leaving by the early morning train. The Archdeacon had charge of the negatives and had promised to let us know as soon as he had deciphered the message.

The mediums did not like their lodgings, so slept at my hotel. I saw them off in the morning, *before any of us knew what the message was*. A day or two later I received from the mediums a duplicate of the message not yet known to them or to myself. But this time the writing was large enough to be read by the naked eye. As Prof. Henslow had requested, the same thing had come on all the plates in differing degrees of distinctness.

This was my first experience of a Crewe skotograph, and it was decisive. As I wrote in the *Psychic Gazette* from notes submitted to Archdeacon Colley at the time, and afterwards read by Prof. Henslow when published, no suspicions could fall either on the mediums, Archdeacon Colley or myself, as not one of us had had the chance of tampering with Prof. Henslow's plate, nor could Prof. Henslow and his photographer have prepared a series of plates for an occasion on which they had no reason to have reckoned.

I wrote a minute account of these early experiments, according to the strictest psychical research methods, and left it with Mr. Wallis, the then editor of *Light*. He did not publish it, and when I returned to England it could not be found. This incident is briefly recorded by Prof. Henslow in *Proofs of the Truths of Spiritualism*, pp. 224-7.

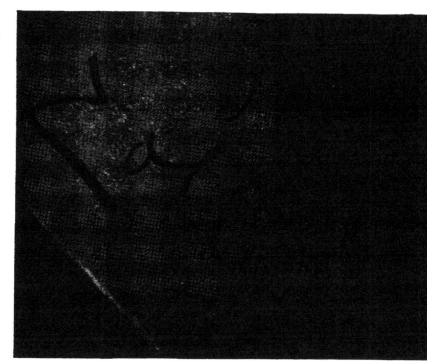

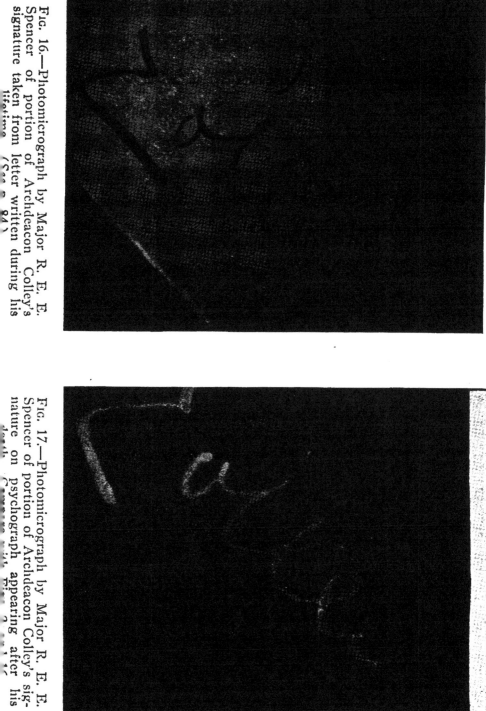

Fig. 16.—Photomicrograph by Major R. E. E. Spencer of portion of Archdeacon Colley's signature taken from letter written during his lifetime. (See p. 84.)

Fig. 17.—Photomicrograph by Major R. E. E. Spencer of portion of Archdeacon Colley's signature on psychograph, appearing after his death. (Compare with Fig. 16, p. 84.)

FIG. 19.—Mr. and Mrs. Harry Walker and two
friends with psychic "...

FIG. 18.—Photograph of Mr. Wm. Walker
with message in the handwriting of Mr.

CHAPTER VIII

EVIDENTIAL AND SCIENTIFIC ASPECTS OF
PSYCHIC PHOTOGRAPHY

BY FRED BARLOW

Hon. Sec. S.S.S.P., Hon. Sec. Birmingham and Midland S.P.R.

No phase of psychical research has been more adversely criticised in the past than psychic photography. This is undoubtedly due to the prevalence of many erroneous ideas on the whole subject.

It is a popular fallacy that it is the easiest thing in the world to fake a "spirit" photograph. Those few photographers who have tried to imitate a genuine psychic effect have usually made the discovery that it is by no means so easy a matter as it appears, even when no restriction is placed on the conditions under which the fake should be produced. When conditions are imposed, similar to those usually obtaining with, say, the Crewe Circle, the difficulty of producing a fraudulent result is enormously increased. Under certain conditions, where suitable precautions are employed and where the sitter has a thorough knowledge of photography, plus an acquaintance with trick methods, even the *possibility* of deception without detection can, for all practical purposes, be ruled out of court. *Under these special conditions, investigators of repute have on many occasions secured successful psychic results.*

Apart altogether from any question of test conditions, however, there are certain results which, *in them-*

[79]

selves, afford definite proof of their genuine nature. I refer to those recognised psychic likenesses obtained by sitters who are quite unknown to the sensitives and who have secured results which could not possibly have been prepared in advance. One such case would be sufficient to establish the reality of psychic photography. It is no exaggeration to say that this has actually occurred on scores of occasions, and, in consequence, *the evidence for the truth of psychic photography is overwhelming.*

It has been said that recognised psychic likenesses exists only in the imagination of the individuals claiming them as such. It is, alas, too true that some well-meaning individuals will see a likeness where none exists. It is, however, equally true that many bigoted sceptics will refuse to acknowledge a likeness that is obvious to the unprejudiced on comparing normal and supernormal photographs. There are two sides to the question of credulity, and I have known sceptics deny the reality of a likeness where the supernormal effect has been an exact (but draped) duplicate of a normal photograph!

We must remember that it may be difficult to recognise a likeness between a normal and supernormal photograph where the subject to us is unknown. Two photographs of the same individual, taken at different periods, will often vary considerably, but those acquainted with that individual can recognise the likeness of each photograph to the original without the slightest difficulty. So in a supernormal photograph: those claiming a likeness between the supernormal effect and some near relative, or friend, who has crossed the border, are in a better position, from their knowledge of that person, to speak with authority on the question of recognition than those who never saw the original. This question of recognised likenesses is a point the critic tries to evade. The reader can judge of the value of this evidence from the few illustrations in this booklet which are typical of *hundreds* of similar results.

The mental attitude of some intelligent people to psychic photography is distinctly curious. They have got the idea fixed into their heads that these photographs *must* be one of two things—"fakes" or "spirits." Naturally enough, in some of the cases that have been reported they find it difficult to believe that such a result could have been produced entirely by a discarnate entity. Therefore they jump to the false conclusion that the result must of necessity have been faked. In a scientific investigation we should first of all concern ourselves with *facts*, without troubling over-much with theories. A very little first-hand investigation will satisfy any unprejudiced individual as to the reality of psychic photography. Having reached that stage such a person will be in a better position to theorise on the cause of the phenomena.

After many years of close concentration on this subject I have arrived at the conclusion that psychic photography differs only in kind and not in degree from other phases of psychic phenomena. *I do not see how we can possibly get away from the fact that many of these photographic effects are produced by discarnate intelligences.* Whilst firmly believing this, I should never be so dogmatic as to claim that *all* supernormal pictures have been produced by discarnate spirits

THE CASE FOR SPIRIT PHOTOGRAPHY

Spirit, whether discarnate or incarnate, to manifest to our material senses must make use of matter—there must be a medium. A medium, or sensitive, is just as essential for psychic photography as for, say, automatic writing. As investigators are aware, in automatic script it frequently happens that along with communications from the "other side" come writings derived from the subconsciousness of the automatist, and such, I am convinced, is often the case in psychic photography.

The subconscious is used to cover a multitude of theories. Certainly it is not an unfeasible explanation in some instances. Let me cite one case, which is typical of many. One of the members of the S.S.S.P.— Mr. Hobbs, of Purley, a keen business man—travelled to Crewe with his wife. They and the Crewe Circle were perfect strangers to each other. Mrs. Hobbs at the time was wearing a locket containing a photograph of their son, who had been killed in the war. This was tucked away out of sight in her blouse. The usual séance was held and to their great delight the visitors secured a picture of their boy. Trickery was impossible. Even supposing Mr. Hope had seen the photograph in the locket there was no time to produce a fraudulent result and foist this upon the alert sitters. A careful examination of the print, however, reveals the fact that the psychic picture is an exact but reversed duplicate of the photograph in the locket. Even the rim of the locket can be clearly seen. This sort of thing has occurred time and again.

The image of the locket would be indelibly impressed on the memory of the mother, and it may well be that in some peculiar way the sensitive proved a medium for the projection of that conscious or subconscious image on to the photographic plate. Such an argument is not to be lightly dismissed, and the fact that the image obtained on the plate may not have been in the conscious mind of the sitter at the time does not necessarily affect the issue. I candidly admit that some such explanation may account for many of these curious effects.

Sometimes the psychic pictures are facsimile copies of magazine covers and pictures no fraudulent medium would ever think of producing, and, like the faces in our dreams, they may come from the subconscious. At the same time, attempts to produce definite conscious thought-pictures, with the co-operation of a photographic medium, have almost always proved abortive in our experiments in this country. Some of the Continental members of the S.S.S.P., however, have concentrated on this line of research and have succeeded in obtaining thoughtgraphs which, more or less, resemble the object on which the thoughts of the subject have been intensely concentrated. These experiments, and, in particular, recent photographic experiments in connection with subjects under hypnosis, are yielding encouraging results.

We must be careful not to overdo the subconscious. It is no self-contained unit, but rather an instrument used in the production of these phenomena. In consequence, it frequently happens that along with communications from the "other side" comes matter derived from the subconsciousness of the sensitive and even from that of the sitter. An investigator obsessed with the idea of fraud will often effectively negative all phenomena by his unconscious action on the mentality of the medium. In these investigations we must use that uncommon faculty of common sense. Common sense tells us that we cannot accept the explanation that *all* psychic photographs are produced by the thoughts of incarnate beings. Whether it agrees with his pet theories or not, the serious student is bound to realise that, sooner or later, other minds are at work distinct from, and often superior in intelligence to, that of either medium or sitter. These intelligences claim to be the spirits of the so-called dead. They substantiate their claims by giving practical proof that they are whom they purport to be.

For example, what better proof of survival could be given by a deceased person than that of a message in his own handwriting, referring to events that happened after his death? Such messages are by no means an unfrequent occurrence. There can be no doubt about the genuineness of the handwriting. Major R. E. E. Spencer has gone to an immense amount of time and trouble in making photomicrographs of normal and supernormal writings for the purpose of comparison. Illustrations are given of two of these photomicrographs. Figure 16 shows a portion of the signature of Archdeacon Colley taken from a letter written by him before death, whilst Figure 17 shows a corresponding portion reproduced from a photographic message received after his death. This message referred to events subsequent to his decease.

Occasionally, in these psychographs, as these written photographic messages are termed, the mentality of the medium or sitters will get in the way, with very curious results. Throughout all these phenomena, however, there is every indication that other influences are at work. Whoever or whatever these intelligences behind the scenes may be, in no uncertain voice they claim to be discarnate souls. Surely *they* are in a better position to form a correct opinion hereon than we material outsiders?

How do the psychic images get on to the plate? Far too much time, in the past, has been lost in attempting to convince those who do not believe (and those who do not *want* to believe), of the genuine nature of psychic photography, and our ignorance of this phenomenon is appalling. The difficulties attending scientific research in this domain are considerable. So far, we can only definitely say that in many instances the psychic figures on the plate are not objective in the same sense as the sitters. The supernormal images have every appearance of having been projected on to the sensitive plate, independently of the lens and camera. In employing several cameras simultaneously, together with a stereo camera, I have only succeeded so far in securing a psychic image on one of the plates exposed.

There are indications that in some cases the psychic effects are printed on to the plate through a psychic equivalent to our normal transparency—in fact, it has come to be known as a psychic transparency. Identical transparency markings are to be found on the plates of photographic sensitives from all parts of the world. These particular markings can clearly be seen over the negative obtained by Mr. Harry Price in his experiment

[85]

THE CASE FOR SPIRIT PHOTOGRAPHY

with Mr. Hope. I am convinced that the effect obtained on this occasion was a genuine psychic result. The possibility of this is freely admitted by Mr. Price. The fact that in nine cases out of ten the psychic images are the same way up as the sitter suggests that the "something" that occurs actually takes place after the plate has been inserted in the dark slide. Such small points as these may eventually play an important part in the final solution of the *modus operandi*.

Now let us return to the object of this book—the question of evidence. Sir Arthur Conan Doyle has dealt so thoroughly, earlier in these pages, with the recent attacks by the S.P.R. and the Magic Circle that I do not propose to refer to them again here at length. As illustrating the impartial attitude of the Society of which I have the honour to be Secretary, however, I would like to say that almost immediately on the publication of these critical reports the matter was discussed by the members of this Society, and it was arranged to subject the whole of the evidence to a thorough investigation. In this connection the S.S.S.P., in conjunction with the B.C.P.S., sought the co-operation of the Society for Psychical Research and the Occult Committee of the Magic Circle.

A proposal was sent to the bodies mentioned expressing the desire of the S.S.S.P. to subject the charges to thorough and impartial investigation, and suggesting that three members from each of these four bodies should form a committee of investigation. The members elected by the S.S.S.P. were Dr. Abraham Wallace, President, Col. C. E. Baddeley, C.M.G., O.G., and Major R. E. E. Spencer, three careful and experienced investigators. For reasons best known to themselves, both the S.P.R. and the Occult Committee of the Magic Circle refused to entertain this suggestion. The reader can draw whatever inference he likes from this uncompromising attitude. To my mind such a refusal is directly opposed to the objects for which the Society for Psychical Research was formed.

A striking example of the persistence of personality is to be found in the case of the late Mr. Wm. Walker, of Buxton. Mr. Walker was the President of the Buxton Camera Club. Being a keen photographer, he took an intense interest in the work of the Crewe Circle and co-operated with them in numerous experiments. He was the first photographer to obtain psychic photographic results in colours (by the Paget process) through the mediumship of his friends.

Shortly before the late Mr. W. T. Stead left this country for his last voyage to America, Mr. Walker saw him in London. Mr. Stead was very interested in the results obtained at Crewe and strongly urged his friend to keep him posted as to future developments. A little while later Mr. Stead was drowned on the ill-fated *Titanic*. On May 6th, 1912, Mr. Walker, in experimenting at Crewe, was surprised and pleased to receive on his plates a message from his friend, which read:

"DEAR MR. WALKER,
"I will try to keep you posted.
"W. T. STEAD."

Two plates had been exposed; both contained the same message, but in one case the writing was reversed and appeared as "mirror writing," as it is called. This result is shown by Figure 18. The writing does not reproduce very clearly, but experts have declared that, beyond all doubt, it is identical with the handwriting of the late W. T. Stead.

Mr. Wm. Walker followed Mr. Stead into the Great Beyond a few years later. Since his death his relatives and friends have received innumerable tokens of his activities on the "other side," in connection with the subject in which he was so interested whilst in the body. The illustration shown by Figure 19 represents a normal photograph of Mr. H. Walker and his wife (son and daughter-in-law) and two friends, with a clearly-defined supernormal likeness of the late Mr. Wm. Walker. This was taken under satisfactory test conditions on February 19th, 1916.

As illustrating the interest Mr. Walker still takes in the Crewe Circle, attention is directed to the psycho-graph shown by Figure 20. This was secured late on Friday evening, July 28th, 1922, and reads (my own punctuation):

"Dear Friends of the Circle,
"I would not spend a moment with the Psychical Research Scty, because they are nothing more nor less than fraud hunters and I want you to come to Buxton for a sitting with Mrs. Walker, 3, Palace Rd., about the 8th 9th of Aug. Then the spirit friends can further demonstrate the wondrous powers which to-day are needed more than ever. Peace be with you.
"Yours faithfully,
"W. WALKER."
"Please inform Henry."

[88]

EVIDENTIAL AND SCIENTIFIC ASPECTS

The postscript refers to Mr. Walker's son, who re-
sides in Crewe. I have examined a number of letters
in the handwriting of Mr. Walker, senior, and find
that the slip in spelling is such that he might make.
A portion of one of these letters is reproduced on Figure
21, and when compared with the psychograph alongside it should leave no doubts in the mind of the reader
as to authorship.

It is perhaps unnecessary to state that the instructions given by Mr. Wm. Walker were carried out to
the letter. The results of the short visit of the Crewe
Circle to Buxton are best described by quoting an extract from a letter I received from Mr. Henry Walker:

"We (Mrs. Buxton, Mr. Hope and myself) went
to Buxton on Wednesday, 9th inst. (August, 1922.
—ED.). Two sittings were held and four exposures
made.

"The first exposure was made on mother, and
gives a message from father to Mrs. Buxton and Mr.
Hope, dealing again with the S.P.R. test and promis-
ing a puzzle.

"The second exposure was made on mother, Mrs.
Marriott (an old friend of ours) and myself, and
shows a very large face of father nearly covering
the three of us.

"I developed each plate carefully and noticed the
psychic light was much more keen than the daylight.

"After a rest of a couple of hours, we held the
second sitting.

"The first plate exposed on mother shows a med-
ley: a good photo of father and a lot of flowers or
foliage and the feathers of a Red Indian friend.

"The second plate only shows a few lights.

"I fancy father's record alone should be sufficient
to satisfy any sensible being. I daresay I can find

[89]

well over twenty psychic results received from him on different occasions, most of them under reasonable test conditions.

(*Signed*) "H. WALKER."

The Crewe Circle invariably place implicit faith in the messages they receive from the other side. These worthy and simple people are very closely in touch with their invisible helpers, who advise them, by means of photographic messages, in their troubles and ailments., Occasionally the advice given has been directly opposed to the wishes of the mediums, but they never hesitate to carry out these instructions, which usually prove that the directing intelligences possess knowledge and foresight far exceeding that of their human instruments.

I can appreciate that some of my readers will experience difficulty in accepting these remarkable statements. When first I heard of these marvellous things I put them down to credulity, exaggeration, and so forth. However, I determined to get at the truth for myself. Nothing less than personal experience would satisfy me. The first psychic photographs I saw did not very greatly impress me. As a photographer, I recognised that I could produce similar results, and with the conceit that comes from ignorance I suggested they were fakes. Even as fakes they were interesting, however, and on inquiring further into the matter I discovered that the conditions under which they had been secured would necessitate smart work on the part of a trickster. Also I was puzzled to understand how photographers of the calibre of Mr. J. Traill Taylor could be easily gulled. Eventually I travelled to Crewe in a rather critical frame of mind, but fully prepared to be fair to the mediums. I received a surprise. The result obtained bore a strong resemblance to myself. It could easily be taken as a twin brother. I had a brother who, when he died, was a little older than myself. I was given practically a free hand in the photographic operations, and was impressed by the faith and honesty of the mediums. To detail all the precautions I took from time to time to eliminate the possibility of conscious and even unconscious deception, in my further experiments, would prove a wearisome business. Suffice it to say that the use of my own apparatus and specially-prepared plates, the dismissal of the medium from the dark room for all the photographic operations, the sharp look-out that was kept for certain known methods of faking, and the conducting of experiments with the mediums in my own home, eventually convinced me, beyond all doubt, of the reality of psychic photography.

I discovered early that the mental attitude of the sitter played an important part in the success or otherwise of the experiment. We know so little of the difficulties that have to be overcome—so little of the laws and conditions governing the production of these wonderful results, that it is essential we should approach the subject with an open mind. We must be sympathetic in our methods of investigation. A medium is sensitive in more senses than one, and a little tact and persuasion will succeed where bullying and blustering will fail.

With the three photographic sensitives most known in this country I have secured remarkable results.

THE CASE FOR SPIRIT PHOTOGRAPHY

Whatever may have happened, or may happen, on other occasions, nothing can in the slightest degree shake my firm conviction that, with these three sensitives, I have secured genuine psychic photographic effects. With Mrs. Deane, in my own home, we secured an excellent picture of my father (see Figure 30). True, Mrs. Deane had the plates beforehand for "magnetising," but that would not enable her to produce an unmistakable likeness of someone she had never seen—a likeness which could not have been produced from any existing photograph, in the very unlikely event of her obtaining such. Moreover it is not essential, in every case, that Mrs. Deane should have the plates beforehand for magnetising. On several occasions, members of the S.S.S.P. have, without Mrs. Deane's knowledge, substituted a fresh unopened packet of plates for the unopened packet she has had with her, without interfering with the success of the experiment.

Mr. Vearncombe has been most successful as a medium for obtaining results on plates in sealed packets. Effectively to test Mr. Vearncombe, I devoted a great deal of time to wrapping and sealing packets which could not possibly be tampered with without leaving some trace of such tampering. Others have done likewise, and on the plates in such packets, which after the most careful scrutiny have revealed no evidence of tampering, we have secured successful results. On one occasion I persuaded a local professional photographer to seal a packet of plates before I handled them. This he did very thoroughly, and then I added my own wrappings and seals and sent the package on to Vearncombe. Within a week the packet was returned intact.

EVIDENTIAL AND SCIENTIFIC ASPECTS

Mr. Frederic Lewis of Birmingham, who co-operated with me in this test, is a technical photographer of more than average ability and his certificate is of value. In this he states:

"I certify that on May 14th, 1920, I wrapped and sealed an unopened packet of Imperial Special Sensitive ¼-plates and handed the packet to Mr. Fred Barlow, who then fixed his own wrappings and seals. Mr. Barlow brought back the packet of plates to me on the morning of May 20th, 1920, and in my presence broke his own wrappings and seals. I then very carefully verified that my own seals and wrappings were intact and am quite convinced that these had not been interfered with. I personally developed the plates in the presence of Mr. Barlow. On two out of the twelve plates in the package distinct negative images of faces developed—one face on one plate and three small faces on another. I can offer no explanation of this result apart from being perfectly satisfied that no trickery or deception was practised.

(*Signed*) "FREDERIC LEWIS."

Could anything be more definite and conclusive than that?

With the Crewe Circle I have had so many tests that it is difficult to select the most stringent. As the well-known Price case of alleged fraud bears on the question of the substitution of dark slides, the following case may be of interest. On this occasion the substitution of dark slides was impossible, for the simple reason that no dark slides were used.

Saying nothing to the members of the Circle beforehand, I took with me to Crewe on November 12th,

[93]

1921, a loaded box camera containing six specially-
marked plates of a size smaller than those usually employed in experiments of this nature. All that Hope
and Mrs. Buxton did was to arch their hands over
this magazine camera whilst one of them flicked the
shutter-catch. Photographic readers will realise that
it is impossible to tamper with the plates in a box
camera, in daylight, without spoiling the lot. To enable the "power" to flow from Mr. Hope on to the
plates, the controlling intelligence stipulated that Mr.
Hope should be allowed to take hold of my right wrist
as I dropped each plate into the developer. Psychic
effects were secured on two out of the six plates under
conditions which, I am convinced, rendered deception
impossible. I have been told that Mr. Hope must have
printed the effects on to the plates by flashlight whilst
he had hold of my wrist. If the critic derives any
comfort from believing that this actually occurred he
is welcome to his belief!

In another evidential case is that already mentioned
by Sir Arthur Conan Doyle of an experiment conducted
by two photographic members of the S.S.S.P. and
myself at Crewe. In this case the camera and slides
employed were brand new and were not examined by
the sensitives until after the sitting. The dark slides
differed from those usually employed by the sensitives.
Neither Mr. Hope nor Mrs. Buxton was in the dark
room for loading the slides or for developing the plates.
The central face of three supernormal faces secured
on this occasion is an undoubted likeness of the father
of one of the sitters. The result was absolutely conclusive to my friends and myself. We emphatically

FIG. 20.—Psychograph in the handwriting of Mr. Wm. Walker obtained at Crewe on July 28th, 1922. Compare with normal handwriting shown

FIG. 21.—Portion of letter written by Mr. Wm. Walker during his lifetime for comparison with psychograph, Fig. 20.

Fig. 23.—Photograph of Mr. Maddocks' first wife for comparison with Fig. 22.

Fig. 22.—Mr. S. Maddocks, Hon. Sec. of the Sheffield and District S.P.R., with psychic photograph of his first wife. Compare with

declare that under the circumstances trickery was impossible.

Since the above was written I have been favoured with further excellent personal proof. On October 7th, 1922, I secured at Crewe several fine photographs of my father. The best were secured on plates exposed in a camera brought by one of three friends who accompanied me. He is an experienced and critical photographer, and was responsible for the whole of the photographic operations. Reference to Figure 31 will show that the psychic face has moved and appears in no less than six different places. This face is very similar to the Deane photo (Figure 30), but by no means absolutely identical.

The next chapter contains a series of abbreviated accounts and reports by investigators in every station of life. For the purpose of this book they are confined to accounts connected with the Crewe Circle. In my capacity of Hon. Secretary to the S.S.S.P. it is my privilege to receive these documents in ever-increasing numbers. I imagine that the most hardened sceptic, occupying a similar position for a few months, would be convinced of the reality of psychic photography by this evidence alone. Knowing it to be true, I look forward with confidence to that day, not far distant, when all this talk of fake and fraud shall be no more and when the psychologist and scientist shall combine the investigation of this vital problem.

CHAPTER IX

THIS concluding chapter contains a number of plain, straight statements from those possessing first-hand knowledge of the Crewe Circle. Such positive and definite evidence is of far more value from an eviden- tial and scientific standpoint than the mere opinions of those who have never investigated. Owing to the exigencies of space it has been necessary to abbreviate most of these accounts and also to omit many others, equally convincing. For evidential reasons each report or contribution contains the full name and address of the communicator.

The Evidence of GEORGE H. LETHEM, ESQ.,
JUSTICE OF THE PEACE FOR THE COUNTY OF THE
CITY OF GLASGOW

I first heard of the Crewe Circle in the autumn of 1918. At that time I was editor of the *Daily Record,* Glasgow, and had made the acquaintance of Mr. Peter Galloway, President of the Glasgow Association of Spiritualists, through an article on spiritualism which he contributed to that paper.

Mr. Galloway told me that the Crewe. Circle were coming to Glasgow, and he invited me to attend their first sitting. This I agreed to do; I bought a packet of quarter-plates at a City shop, took note of the wrapper markings and kept the packet safe, with the cover un- broken.

[96]

CONCLUSIVE PROOF

My wife accompanied me to the sitting, which was held in a large, well-lighted attic room some distance from the house where the members of the Circle were lodging. I saw them arrive, saw them unpack their photographic outfit, and saw them borrow a dark cloth (which I examined) for use as a background. Obtaining permission, I examined the camera, the slide, the lens, the bellows (for pin-holes) and all the accessories, without finding anything suspicious. I treated the sitting as a test and took every step, so far as I knew, to provide against conscious or unconscious deception.

Including Mr. Hope and Mrs. Buxton, there were nine or ten people present. To all of these, except Mr. Galloway, I was quite unknown, and I was introduced simply as a "friend."

I had time to complete my examination—in which I included the little adjoining dark room—before the proceedings began. All present then sat round a table, on which my packet of plates was laid within my reach and in my sight. There were hymns and a prayer, then the packet was lifted and held for a few seconds between Mr. Hope's hands, with the hands of all the others—my own included—above and below. The packet, which was never out of my sight, was then returned to me and I satisfied myself by the markings that it was mine, that the wrapper was intact, and that, therefore, there could have been no tampering with the plates.

Putting the unopened packet in my pocket, I followed Mr. Hope into the dark room, taking with me the slide from the camera. In the dark room Mr. Hope stood in the far corner and I stood close by the door, leaving a clear space between us. Mr. Hope said, in explanation of this arrangement, that he did not want to touch the plates but only to see that I handled them properly.

Taking the packet from my pocket, I broke the cover, extracted two plates and put the packet back in my pocket. Keeping the plates within Mr. Hope's view

but quite out of his reach, I wrote my name on each of
them and put them into the slide, which I carried out of
the room before handing it to Mr. Hope. Up to this
point, Mr. Hope had quite certainly not touched the ·
plates. Having seen the slide placed in the camera, I ·
sat down beside my wife, facing the lens.

The camera had been previously focussed and an
exposure was made—Mr. Hope standing on the right
and Mrs. Buxton on the left and joining hands (Mr.
Hope's left, Mrs. Buxton's right) above the camera.·
In this attitude Mr. Hope pressed the pneumatic bulb
with his right hand and so made the exposure, which
was longer than for an ordinary photograph. Then the
slide was turned and a second exposure was made on
other two members of the party.

When the second exposure was completed, Mr. Hope
took the slide out of the camera, carried it into the dark
room, and emptied the plates into my hands in front of
the red glass window. Making sure that my signature
was on each of the plates, I placed them in a shaded
receptacle, signed other two plates and put them into
the slide with the same precautions as before. Then,
seeing Mr. Hope out of the room, I shut the door and
stood before it whilst two other exposures were made.
Re-entering the dark room, I received the plates from
the slide as before and proceeded to develop the four
plates with material supplied by Mr. Hope, who remained in the room but stood as far from the developing dish as possible and left the whole of the handling
to me.

Standing before the red window, I saw the images
come up on the plates and noticed that on three of them
there were figures other than the ordinary representa-
tions of the sitters. When development was finished, I
carried the plates from the dark room and, before anyone else was allowed to touch them, I examined them
individually and satisfied myself beyond doubt that they
were the four identical plates on which I had written

my name and that the normal figures on these plates corresponded with the four exposures I had seen made.

That each of the four plates bore my signature, clear and characteristic, I accepted as proof that these were the plates I had placed in the slide and no others, for it was impossible that my signature could have been forged: therefore, I reasoned, there had been no substitution of prepared plates.

Looking through the negatives, I could see that, in addition to the normal figures of the sitters, there were distinct "extras" on three of the plates, each "extra" being distinct in form from the others.

On No. 1 plate—that for which my wife and I had been the sitters—there was the clear representation of a face looking out from an arched veil. This "extra" was superimposed on the image of the sitters and partially obscured them, as if the "something" it represented had come between them and the lens.

As soon as the plate was dry, a rough print was obtained by placing a sheet of printing paper over the negative and holding it up to the window, through which the sun was shining. That rough print showed the normal figures and the "extra" as they were afterwards printed by Mr. Hope.

Five possibilities are, therefore, ruled out in seeking to account for this particular "extra":

1. The plates were not faked before exposure.
2. There was no substitution of plates.
3. There was no double exposure.
4. There was no double printing.
5. The plate was not faked after development.

As soon as the rough proof of plate No. 1 was obtained, the face of the "extra" was recognised by my wife and myself as an unmistakable likeness of our elder son, who had been killed in the war, and this recognition was corroborated fully and completely

[99]

later on by other members of the family, and is there-fore beyond dispute.

In considering this likeness and its recognition, I take note of certain facts, namely: (1) That Mr. Hope did not know me and did not know my son, or even that I had a son; (2) that neither Mr. Hope nor anyone in the room, save my wife and myself, had ever seen my son, and that it is unlikely that any one of them had seen his photographs; and (3) that although the like-ness is unmistakable, the image of the face is not a reproduction of any normal photograph.

In view of these facts, it seemed to me then, and seems to me still, that it was quite impossible that Mr. Hope could have consciously produced that likeness either by skill or trick or both.

I was afterwards present at several of Mr. Hope's sittings and was allowed on at least two other occasions to accompany him into the dark room and to watch the whole of his procedure. I kept a keen lookout for tricks—with many of which I was acquainted, but I saw none.

Also I have discussed the details many times with photographic experts and I have read the accusations brought against Mr. Hope, and I am quite satisfied that —whatever may have happened on other occasions— none of the suggestions of trickery put forward can account for the "extras" I have described, and particu-larly for that in which I am most directly interested.

(*Signed*) GEORGE H. LETHEM.

Hazeldene,
    Harehills Lane,
        Leeds.

CONCLUSIVE PROOF

The Evidence of W. G. MITCHELL, ESQ.,

OF DARLINGTON

(Mr. Mitchell is a Vice-President of the S.S.S.P., and President of the Darlington Photographic Society. He is a photographer and investigator of considerable experience.)

I first came in touch with Mr. Hope and Mrs. Buxton at Crewe. My second meeting with these good people was at Middlesbrough, where they were spending a holiday. I have thus had an opportunity of experimenting in the atmosphere of their own séance-room and studio, and also under the improvised conditions of a friend's residence.

The subject of supernormal photography was not entirely new to me. I had met Mr. Edward Wyllie, the "spirit" photographer, when in Ireland, and watched his operations almost daily during his fortnight's sojourn in that country. I subjected him to the most stringent and ingenious tests that I could devise. As founder and president of a photographic society, I was fully alive to all the possibilities of faking, but was quite satisfied that I had removed from Mr. Wyllie any opportunity to indulge in photographic legerdemain. With all my caution, results persisted. All the ordinary laws of photography, as far as I understood them, were upset and violated.

But to get back to the Crewe Circle. I had arranged with a friend who was at that time editor-manager of an important Northern newspaper to visit Crewe for the purpose of meeting the Crewe Circle. As brother members of a psychical research society, we desired to add to our experiences. Having taken the precaution of purchasing plates locally and following the usual recommendation of carrying them in close proximity to the body, we looked forward to our journey. The appointed day arrived, but no day in modern history could have been more unsuitable or less conducive to good results. It was December 16th, 1914, and the news tapped out over the "private wire" was most disquieting; the Huns were shelling Scarborough and West Hartlepool. My friend realised that it was impossible for him to desert his editorial chair, and he hurriedly gave me his box of plates. I met Mr. William Walker, of Buxton, *en route,* and together we journeyed to Crewe. A short devotional service was held in the kitchen of Mrs. Buxton's home, during which I was informed that only one box of plates could be dealt with. I selected the box purchased by my absent friend and expressed a desire that some result should be given that would give him satisfaction and conviction. I was instructed that four plates would be dealt with and that I could select any particular four I desired from the box; I named the third and fourth, ninth and tenth. This selection secured two pairs of plates that would be packed film to film, and would probably be hinged together with emulsion.

The unsealed box was then placed on the centre of the table, and as it bore a rubber stamp impression of the firm from which it was purchased I am quite satisfied that there was no substitution of boxes. Mr. Hope then, insisted that I should dismantle his camera. This I did most thoroughly, giving special attention to the dark slides, lens and shutter.

Having placed the dark slides in my pocket, we entered the dark room, where I unpacked the box, selecting the particular plates decided upon, wrote my initials across the corner of each, placed them in the two double back dark slides and placed the remainder of the plates together with the dark slides in my pocket. We adjourned to the studio, where Hope allowed me to choose my position in relation to the background. Mr. Walker sat in the chair, I focussed the portrait on the focussing screen of the camera, placed the dark slide in position and left all ready for making the exposure.

I then went and took a seat beside Mr. Walker. Mr. Hope manipulated the lens cap with one hand and with his other clasped Mrs. Buxton's, thus forming an arc over the bellows of the camera. After the first plate was exposed I went to the camera, closed the dark slide and reversed it, then sat for the second exposure.

The third plate was next used. Mrs. Buxton asked me to place the dark slide containing the only unexposed plate on her forehead, this I did for about ten seconds.

I then retired with Mr. Hope to the dark room, where I personally developed the four plates. On three out of the four supernormal effects flashed up, and after fixing in the hypo-bath we brought them out to the light for examination.

Plate No. 1, in addition to the normal image, showed a lengthy message of exceedingly minute copperplate writing, too small to read without the aid of the magnifying glass. I could just discern that there were Greek characters intermingled with other languages, including English.

No. 2 plate bore only the normal image.

No. 3 plate showed the supernormal figure of a lady draped in some material of fine texture, standing by my side.

No. 4 plate, the one held on Mrs. B.'s forehead, showed a well-defined face of a lady.

The long message on No. 1 contained 145 words, and was written in a jumble of languages, English, Greek, French, and Latin, and concluded thus: "And now, friends, we have given you this advice in mixed languages, so that it will help to support the claim that the unlearned of to-day possess the same powers as the humble fishermen of biblical history. We thank you for the common-sense way in which you have met us. . . ." etc. It was quite two years before I was able to get the Greek portion translated. I eventually met a young Greek, a student of Armstrong College, New-

THE CASE FOR SPIRIT PHOTOGRAPHY

castle, who told me that it was a very ancient style of Greek. The message, when translated, was quite intelligible to me.

No. 3 plate, with supernormal portrait, proved to be undeniably the portrait of the deceased mother of the wife of my friend. On comparing it with a life portrait it left no doubt in the mind of any reasonable person. The portrait on No. 4 plate I cannot recognise.

I have a profound conviction that Mr. Hope is a genuine medium, honest and straightforward, and it would take a great deal to shake my confidence in his integrity. I have followed his operations for years, and find them a fruitful source of instruction. It is only those who have experimented in "fake" effects who can realise the difficulties, and with a knowledge of photography I challenge any professional or amateur photographer to produce anything approaching the same effects under any conditions. They find it absolutely impossible under the *same* conditions.

It is unthinkable that Mr. and Mrs. Buxton would co-operate, aid and abet in a continuous fraud on the widowed wife, the sorrowing parent.

(*Signed*) W. G. MITCHELL.

3, *Harewood Terrace,*
Darlington.

An Account by J. WILLIAMS, ESQ.,

PHOTOGRAPHIC SPECIALIST, OF THE PORTLAND STUDIO, RHYL

It is with the greatest pleasure that I add my testimony to the truthfulness and absolute sincerity of Mr. Hope and Mrs. Buxton.

They have been known to me for several years; altogether no less than six times I have had sittings with them. In every case they have allowed me every facility to eliminate any possible fraud, which as a photogra-

[104]

pher of nearly fifty years' experience, I was eager to discover.

One experience with the Crewe Circle was this: at one sitting I was asked what plate I would choose from a packet of twelve plates; it was decided on the fourth from the top of the packet. The camera was *not* used; Mr. Hope and I entered the dark room and only myself touched the plates during development. On the fourth plate was a message from the late Archdeacon Colley. This negative I have by me and anyone wishing to see same can do so with pleasure.

No one could wish for a better test than this; no one but myself touched the plates at any time during the sitting. The plates I brought with me, tied with special knots to prevent any opening of the packet or substituting of another packet.

(Signed) JNO. WILLIAMS.

Portland Studio,
Rhyl.

The Testimony of JOSEPH HIGGINBOTTOM, ESQ.,

VICE-PRESIDENT OF THE SHEFFIELD AND DISTRICT SOCIETY
FOR PSYCHICAL RESEARCH

(*An account of a surprise visit in which the sitter secured a likeness of his mother, of whom no normal, photograph is in existence.*)

. am pleased to have this opportunity of adding my testimony to the honesty of Mr. Wm. Hope of the Crewe Circle.

Herewith I enclose a psy ic photograph of my mother. [Not reproduced.—ED.] It has been freely recognised by those who, knew her. Such is my confidence in Mr. Hope that I cannot allow myself to imagine for a moment that with his extraordinary gift, in conjunction with Mrs. Buxton he would allow him-

self to be led astray or deviate from the path of recti-
tude under any circumstances.

(*Signed*) J. HIGGINBOTTOM.

Lees House,
  Norton Lees,
    Sheffield.

————

Proof from MRS. E. PICKUP,

OF 40, WATERLOO ROAD, BURNLEY LANCS.

(*A strongly evidential case which describes how
the sitter visited the Crewe Circle as an absolute
stranger and without even an appointment, and
secured a striking likeness of her deceased husband. (See Figs. 28 and 29.) Extract from an
original letter to Mr. Hope.*)

No words of mine can express my gratitude to you
since receiving the photos this morning. The extra one
is my dear husband, and just as I prayed he might come
—an exact copy of the one I had at home and the one
I liked best. Every detail is so clear and correct, even
to the dimple in the chin. What could be more convincing, when I came to you an absolute stranger and
without even an appointment?

That visit will remain imprinted on my memory as
one of the brightest days in my life. I am sure after
such evidence as this and the way in which you carried
out your work, I need never suffer the pangs of loneli-
ness again, because I believe that God has taken him to
a higher sphere. He will still guide me and watch over
me so long as I do my part by keeping in touch with
God and His divine laws.

I don't know that I could ask for anything more.
My cup is full and overflowing. I trust that others who
come to you may get as good results, that they, too, may
know the joy and happiness it brings.

(*Signed*) E. PICKUP.

CONCLUSIVE PROOF

From MRS. RISKER,

LATE OF DARLASTON

(An excellent case, in which the sitter secured an undoubted likeness of her husband. A number of questions were submitted to Mrs. Risker, and her replies are given hereunder.)

I have great pleasure in answering the questions you ask.

Question No. 1.—If there is the slightest doubt concerning "extra"?

None whatever.

Question No. 2.—Whether Mr. Hope or any one connected with the Crewe Circle knew Mr. Risker before his death, or had seen any photograph of him prior to visiting Crewe for this sitting?

No. The first time I ever knew of Mr. Hope or the Crewe Circle was through an article written by Miss Stead in *Nash's Magazine* during the latter part of 1916 (after my husband's death, which occurred August 15th, 1916).

Question No. 3.—In what manner did I get into touch with Crewe Circle?

The article which Miss Stead wrote appealed to me, and knowing Miss Stead (by repute) to be a straightforward woman, the thought came, "Here apparently is a tangible proof of the after-life." Thereupon I did not rest until I found out the address. Some weeks later, a lady from Runcorn who knew nothing of me gave me the address of Mr. Hope.

Since above I have paid six visits and have had nine results—seven "extras" and two "skotographs"; upon five visits I have taken my own plates from Darlaston.

(Signed) M. C. RISKER.

Late of Bilston Street,
Darlaston.

[107]

THE CASE FOR SPIRIT PHOTOGRAPHY

An Expression of Opinion from LADY GREY
OF FALLODEN

I am perfectly ready to adhere to my conviction that
I have obtained evidence of supernormal activities
through the mediumship of the Crewe Circle, and this
I would maintain however conclusively they may have
been convicted of fraud on other occasions.

(*Signed*) PAMELA GREY.

Wilsford Manor,
Salisbury.

The Evidence of H. BLACKWELL, ESQ.,

A VICE-PRESIDENT OF THE S.S.S.P.

(*Mr. Blackwell is one of the pioneers in the
history of psychic photography. His experiences
have been quite exceptional. This description
tells how he secured a photograph of a recently
deceased sister.*)

With great pleasure I give my experience of the good
work done through the Crewe mediums. In April,
1920, having fixed an appointment with Mr. Hope for
a certain hour at the B.C.P.S., I was there to time with
an unopened box of plates. Of the four plates exposed
I found upon development that only two had any
psychic results.

These appeared to consist of several faint faces
merging one into the other. From the wet negatives I
could not recognise any of the features, so asked for
prints to be sent on in due course.

When the prints came to hand I was delighted to
recognise the face of my sister, but repeated five times,
as if in her agitation she could not concentrate sufficiently and had moved during the exposure.

CONCLUSIVE PROOF

She appeared as in her final illness two years previously, when I had gone down into the country to bid "good-bye."

As a testimony to the value of psychic photography I may mention that through the mediumship of Mr. R. Boursnell, in London, and of Mr. W. M. Keeler, in Washington, I have received portraits of my grandfather, mother, two sisters and several of my nieces. A number of friend have also been taken in London after promises given in Canada and elsewhere.

About twelve years ago, thanks to a personal friend who then possessed wonderful materialising power, I was enabled to obtain, using four cameras simultaneously, excellent photographs of my father, mother, niece and several friends. They manifested for the express purpose of being taken, and in each instance the medium shows by the side of the spirit visitor. The experiments were conducted in my house and in presence of witnesses.

(Signed) H. BLACKWELL.

43, Brownswood Road,
Finsbury Park, N. 4.

The Testimony of W. C. PUGH, ESQ.,

OF MIDDLESBROUGH

(A straight statement by an investigator who has secured many recognised psychic photographic results, through the Crewe Circle, in his own home.)

It is a number of years since I first sat with the Crewe Circle, and I have sat with them quite a dozen times since, and on each occasion I have received convincing proof of the genuineness of their phenomena. I have beside me quite a collection of photographs taken by them, and each photo has a message of its own; some contain extras of friends who have passed on, and others contain messages from interested friends beyond the grave. The extras on practically all my photos have been recognised by relatives and friends.

I enclose copy of one of these with two extras which have been readily recognised by all my friends as my father and mother, both of whom had passed on before I met the Crewe Circle. I also enclose copies of original photos for comparison. [Not reproduced.—ED.]

My opportunities for testing the genuineness of the Crewe Circle's work have been unique because they have taken over a hundred photos in my house in Middlesbrough. When they have spent a few days here they have lived with us. My wife and I made all the arrangements for their visit, and entertained them during their stay. Applications for sittings were made to us and we fixed them up. In the vast majority of cases the Crew Circle had never seen the sitters till they arrived at their appointed times. In many cases they never saw them again. Yet their success has been phenomenal. Many have received photos with extras which they recognised at sight. Others have taken them home and had them recognised by friends or other members of their families.

The Circle brought no plates with them. Each sitter provided his or her own. My sitting-room was the studio. My bath-room was the developing room. Unused plates were left behind when the Circle went away, and my lad, who has a camera, has been supplied with a stock of plates for use amongst his friends.

To those of us who know the members of the circle so well, some of the statements appearing in the Press have been very amusing. The idea of Mr. Hope beating the conjurers at their own game is too ridiculous for words. Expert photographers who have had experience of Mr. Hope's methods must also have been greatly amused.

FIG. 24.—Photograph of Mrs. R. Foulds, of Sheffield, with psychic photograph of her mother, obtained under good test conditions.

FIG. 25.—Photograph of Mrs. Foulds' mother for comparison with psychic effect on Fig. 24.

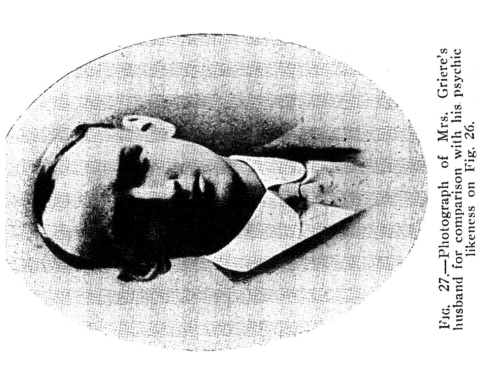

FIG. 27.—Photograph of Mrs. Griere's husband for comparison with his psychic likeness on Fig. 26.

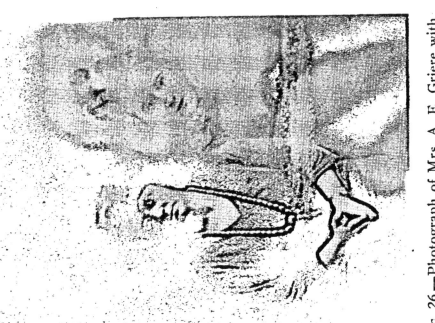

FIG. 26.—Photograph of Mrs. A. E. Griere with psychic likeness of husband and father. The sitter was a total stranger to the Crewe Circle. Compare the lower face with Fig. 27. (See p. 127.)

CONCLUSIVE PROOF

Then there is the question of motive. Let me state that *the Crewe Circle have never had one penny piece out of their various visits to Middlesboro'*. We charged sufficient from each sitter to pay railway expenses only, nothing more. We paid for the railway tickets, that was all. Where on earth was the incentive for these people to leave their homes to come here to deceive us? One's sense of humour must have been neglected if they cannot see that the whole of the charges are too funny for words.

THAT THE PHENOMENA ARE GENUINE I AM CONVINCED. What is behind the phenomena is another matter, and does not enter into the present question.

If the scientists care to continue to drag on behind plain common-sense people let them do so. I have scores of good friends who have had that experience which no scientist can take from them, and I prefer to accept their opinions, along with my own experience, rather than listen to those people whose one desire seems to be to bolster up preconceived ideas.

The world would be better for some more people as honest as are the members of the Crewe Circle.

(*Signed*) WILLIAM COWELL PUGH.

61, *St. Paul's Road,*
Middlesbrough.

An Account by MRS. MARGARET ELLINOR

(A description of three remarkable recognised likenesses obtained by a lady photographer.)

I am anxious to help to prove the truth of psychic photography, and with this end in view I am sending herewith three photographs taken by Mr. Hope, of Crewe, under test conditions, which contain recognised "extras." [Not reproduced.—ED.]

Might I say that in the first place I was extremely

[111]

sceptical, having some knowledge of photography. Even after myself obtaining a "psychograph" I was still in a doubtful frame of mind, and attended the British College of Psychic Science to gather further evidence.

In this way I came into contact with Mr. Hope and Mrs. Buxton, and by and by arranged through the agency of Mrs. McKenzie, of the College, to have a test sitting with Mr. Hope. The results of this sitting, quite apart from any subsequent sittings, provided what to my mind were conclusive proofs of Mr. Hope's gifts and absolute integrity.

Enclosed are four photographs marked. All these were taken under the most stringent test conditions. I took with me some plates which had previously been marked secretly by a second party (a sceptic). These plates were then put into the slide by Mr. Hope in my presence; the slide was never for a moment out of my observation and I subsequently followed every manipulation.

In the case of the photographs (1) and (2) the extra is of my father. An old original photograph of my father is enclosed. It will be observed that the extras give a view from a different angle to the original in each case. My father was unknown to Mr. Hope —there were no photographs of my father available to Mr. Hope—my father passed over when I was nine years of age.

In photograph (3) the extra is of my father-in-law, an original of whom is enclosed. My husband's father has been passed over seven years, and no photograph of him could be available to Mr. Hope.

CONCLUSIVE PROOF

Photograph (4) was taken at another sitting at my home. It is especially interesting inasmuch as the extra thereon was unrecognised at the time. After a lapse of time, through incidents I need not explain, I obtained a clue to the identity of the "extra." Finally I was able to ascertain that the "extra" was one of my girlhood's friends who has now been passed on many years. I was able to secure an old original photograph, which is enclosed.

Having been a sceptic myself, I can sympathise with those who find it difficult to credit these puzzling phenomena. At the same time, I suggest that Mr. Hope is entitled to the sympathetic treatment and fair dealing that should be accorded to anyone who brings forward evidence in support of the super-physical.

(Signed) Margaret Ellinor.

77, Atlantic Road,
Brixton, S.W. 9.

From SAMUEL MADDOCKS, ESQ.,

HON. SECRETARY OF THE SHEFFIELD AND DISTRICT SOCIETY
FOR PSYCHICAL RESEARCH

(*The psychic effect secured by Mr. Maddocks on the occasion of the third sitting described hereunder is shown by fig. 22. A normal photograph of the late Mrs. Maddocks is given for comparison [fig. 23].*)

I am absolutely convinced that Mr. Hope and Mrs. Buxton are transparently honest and honourable, most reverent in their Circle meetings, and their only desire

[113]

is to give comfort and consolation to those who have lost a loved one. To impute fraud or trickery to them wounded me to the quick.

After several months' waiting I obtained three sittings (with three extras) as follows:

1st Sitting.—To my great surprise the "extra" was not my first wife, but the following message:

'Kind friends, we are glad to meet you and for the benefit of your friend of the Psychic Research Society we are giving this message, so that he may understand that, given the right conditions, these works can be done, and we ask you for our dear medium's sake, to speak of it as you find it. God bless you."

2nd Sitting.—This "extra" was quite unknown to me, but on reaching home (Sheffield) my second wife (clairvoyant) exclaimed, "Why, that's the same face I've seen in our bedroom nearly every night."

3rd Sitting.—The "extra" was my first wife at last! I recognised it instantly, also relatives and friends, as a very good picture of what she looked like at the end of twenty months' agony from cancer. All her teeth were extracted during her illness on the advice of a London physician, and that accounts for the sunken appearance of the mouth. (See Figure 22.)

The normal photo was taken several years previously. (See Figure 23.)

(Signed) SAMUEL MADDOCKS.
Supt. Royal Blind School,
Broomhill,
Sheffield.

[114]

CONCLUSIVE PROOF

The Testimony of JAS. P. SKELTON, ESQ.,

OF BELFAST

(The account tells how Mr. Skelton obtained a photograph of his mother, and how later, with two friends, he was present when the famous message from the late Dr. W. J. Crawford was obtained on a photographic plate of their own, under strict test conditions. See figs. 3 and 4.)

I have known Mr. Hope for four or five years now, and have sat with him about a dozen times as well as being closely associated during his and Mrs. Buxton's two visits to Belfast.

On January 4th, 1922, my mother passed to the higher life. I was summoned to Blackburn on Saturday, January 28th, 1922, and as I could not return to Belfast sooner than the Monday night, I decided to make a visit to Crewe with the hope that I might get her photograph. I wrote to Mr. Hope and made an appointment for the Monday morning, January 30th, 1922, and received his reply agreeing. On the night before I crossed to England, we held a brief circle at home, and by means of a small table, my mother manifested. I told her of my intention of going to Crewe and the time that I would be sitting, and she signified that she would do her best to get through. I arrived in Crewe on the day arranged (about 10 a.m.), and found that Mrs. Buxton was ill in bed and could not sit. Naturally I was much disappointed. Mr. Hope noticing it, said, "Never mind, we will sit without her and do the best we can." Mrs. Buxton's daughter sat in her place, Mr. Hope and myself completed the circle. The usual methods were adopted. The packet of plates which I bought in Crewe about five minutes before I reached 144, Market Street were lying on the table during the course of the sitting in full view of all. Mr. Hope and I then proceeded to the dark room, where I initialled the second two plates in the packet, and loaded the slide with them. Never once did Mr. Hope touch them. Miss Buxton and Mr. Hope arranged the camera, etc., after which I handed Mr. Hope the slide. He exposed the two plates and I afterwards developed them myself. On the first was the face of my mother, just as she appeared a few days prior to her death. The plate was hurriedly dried and a print was made for me to take with me, both Mr. Hope and Mrs. Buxton, who knew her recognised it at once. Everyone at home who knew her recognised it immediately, one gentleman saying, "I don't know anything about spiritualism, but if you want an independent testimony, I am prepared to go on any platform and testify to this being your mother's photograph." To me the remarkable thing was, that it was secured exactly twenty-six days after her death. To say Mr. Hope tricked, substituted plates, or in any way defrauded, is puerile.

On a previous occasion I secured a photograph of an old friend of our family who died when I was a boy. It was not recognised for a week after getting it, and then only by chance. I compared an original photograph of her and it proved the identity up to the hilt.

My most recent experience was the securing of the now famous "Crawford" message signed by himself.

CONCLUSIVE PROOF

Mr. J. W. Gillmour, Mr. S. G. Donaldson and myself, all of Belfast, were travelling to the Conferences of the S.N.U., Ltd., in London, and we decided to break our journey at Crewe. Mr. Gillmour bought a packet of ordinary Imperial quarter-plates from Mr. John Bell, of Garfield Street, Belfast, on Thursday, June 29th, 1922, telling Mr. Bell the purpose for which they were required. Mr. Bell parcelled it up and sealed with wax. We crossed to Liverpool same night. Mrs. Crawford also crossed over with us and we travelled together to Crewe, Mrs. Crawford went on to London and we went to see Mr. Hope, arriving there about 10.30 a.m. The usual sitting was arranged, Mr. Gillmour produced the sealed packet, and we all saw the seal was unbroken. It was then broken and the packet was seen to be intact as it came from Mr. Bell's shop. The unopened packet was held between the hands of all present. Mr. Donaldson then took the packet and proceeded with Mr. Hope to load the slides in the dark room, Mr. Donaldson alone handled the plates from beginning to end. We were all photographed together at first, and then separately. The first plate exposed shews a message from Dr. Crawford. With Mr. Gillmour as a sitter there appears an (as yet) unknown face. With Mr. Donaldson there was no psychic effect. With myself a bright light appeared. We were all present at the development and at no time did Mr. Hope touch the plates. Mr. Donaldson did all the work under our careful scrutiny. The result was a surprise to us all. (See Figures 2 and 4.)

We are, however, mutually agreed that it is a *bona*

fide message from Dr. Crawford in his own handwriting, with which I am well acquainted.

(*Signed*) JAS. P. SKELTON.

651, *Lisborn Road,*
Balmoral,
Belfast.

From MISS ESTELLE STEAD

During the last seven or eight years I have had several sittings with the Crewe Circle, and can state truly that I have always found both Mr. Hope and Mrs. Buxton most anxious to have me examine the dark room, the camera, the slides, the room in which the photographs were taken, and had I wished to examine anything else I am sure they would have agreed to my doing so.

At some sittings I have had no results, whilst at others the results have been excellent.

The very first time I visited Crewe I bought a box of plates in London and took it with me. Mr. Hope never handled the box at all excepting in my presence, and we obtained two excellent pictures of my father. During that same visit I bought a box of plates in Crewe, neither Mr. Hope nor Mrs. Buxton had any idea at which shop I bought it. I sealed the box and took it with me to 144, Market Street. I held it in my hands until we, Mr. Hope, Mrs. Buxton, Mr. Harry Walker, at whose house I was staying, and myself— were seated round the table. I then placed the box on the table, where it remained visible to all, as the room was well lighted by gas, whilst we held the little service usually held by the Crewe Circle. We all then placed our hands under and over the box and held it in this way for a little while. I then placed the bottom of the box against Mrs. Buxton's forehead and then held it between my hands whilst instructions were given, through Mr. Hope, to the effect that I should go into the dark room with him, unseal the box myself, take out the bottom plate and the plate next to it. I was told to take particular note as to which was the bottom plate. I was instructed to develop the two plates in Mr. Hope's presence, but not to allow him to touch them until I had developed them. Note, the box was not unsealed until we went into the dark room, and the plates were never exposed to the light at all.

Nothing appeared on the bottom plate, nor was there any sign of fogging. On the other plate were two messages, one in Archdeacon Colley's handwriting and one in Mr. William Walker's handwriting, together with a faint outline of my father's face.

About one year after receiving the above I went up to Crewe with Miss Scatcherd. I had previously, without saying a word to Miss Scatcherd or anyone, made an engagement with my brother Will, who passed over in 1907, to meet me there and give his picture if he could manage to do so. Miss Scatcherd thought I wanted a picture of my father or a message from him. I do not think either Mr. Hope or Mrs. Buxton knew of my brother's existence, and even if they did they certainly had no means of getting hold of his photograph. I took my own plates from town. On the very first plate exposed by brother's face appears between Miss Scatcherd and myself.

During a visit the Crewe Circle paid to the "W. T.

Stead" Bureau in Baker Street in 1919, at my father's request I took my mother to have a sitting with them without advising them beforehand as to who it was I was bringing. I took my own plates, put them in the slides myself and stood over Mr. Hope whilst he developed the plates after the sitting. On the plate exposed on my mother alone there appears a very good picture of my father.

(*Signed*) E. W. STEAD.

5, *Smith Square,*
S.W. 1.

The Evidence of MRS. ELLEN JONES,

OF KEMPSTON

(*Mrs. Jones relates how on two occasions she obtained an excellent likeness of her deceased husband. The second photograph referred to shows a remarkable likeness on comparison with a normal photograph.*)

I had a sitting at Crewe, about four years ago, and again this last March. Success attended both sittings. The March sitting took place in my own house; Mr. Hope and Mrs. Buxton stayed with us a couple of days and we got a photo with three "extras" on one plate. We consider the last one a perfect likeness of my husband just as he was before his last illness. The first was very good, only rather too much like what he was at the time of passing over, so, you see, it was rather painful, but a truthful likeness. My son was with Mr. Hope the whole time he developed the plates. He

CONCLUSIVE PROOF

knows quite a lot about photography, and we used our own plates.

(*Signed*) ELLEN JONES.

Rees Cottage,
Kempston.
Beds.

From THE REV. G. VALE OWEN

I have had several sittings with Mr. Wm.. Hope and Mrs. Buxton at Crewe. I will briefly relate one experience.

In 1910 I was just dropping off to sleep when I saw, in the far corner of the room, a beautiful girl's face smiling at me. It slowly disappeared sideways behind a screen. I wondered who the owner was. It was slightly oval, radiant with joy, and the eyes were laughing at me with just a touch of roguish enjoyment at my perplexity. There was a certain efflorescence permeating it, a light which did not proceed from an exterior object, but which seemed to be one with the substance of which the face was composed. But it was not a mask. It was a living face.

About eight years later I saw the same face again, this time about six inches from my own. On this second occasion there came into my mind, as if intentionally projected there, the name "Ruby." Ruby is my daughter who passed away at the age of fifteen months in 1896.

In August, 1917, my wife and I paid a visit to the Crewe Circle. On one of the negatives appeared the face I had already seen clairvoyantly. It was not full-face, as I had seen it on the two previous occasions, but

[121]

in profile. This disposes of the theory that it might have been a thought-form of my own.

Later on, we were having a talk with this spirit-child of ours in our own home at Orford, and I took the opportunity to ask her if it was she who had managed to get her picture on the plate at Crewe. Her reply was: "I don't know, daddy. I was there and tried to. I should love to have done it. Did I?" My answer was that I was satisfied that she had done so.

I also asked her why it was in profile and she said it was in order that she might shew her hair. Even when she passed away as a baby her abundant light-brown hair was an exceptional feature. On the photograph it was also conspicuous.

I am satisfied that the picture is the likeness of my daughter Ruby. We have received more than one description of her as she appears in the spirit life and this portrait tallies with these descriptions.

I am at one with several of my friends who have sat with them in their conviction that there is no trickery used, by these mediums in the production of results obtained.

On all my visits to Crewe I have been struck with the transparent honesty and earnestness of both Mr. Hope and Mrs. Buxton. The only conclusion to which I can come is that they are out for the sole purpose of helping others with their rare gift, at great cost to their own comfort and convenience. Personally I am grateful to them for their self-sacrificing service.

(*Signed*) G. Vale Owen.

Orford Vicarage,
Warrington.

CONCLUSIVE PROOF

The Testimony of F. J. TWELVES, ESQ.,

OF MANCHESTER

Having had well over twenty sittings with Mr. Hope and Mrs. Buxton of the Crewe Circle, as well as intimate acquaintance of sittings of close friends, I have no hesitation in expressing absolute conviction of the genuineness of the results obtained.

With the exception of photographs of our own son, I cannot say that many were undoubtedly recognised. We have, however, had many photographs of our boy about which there could be no doubt on the part of anybody who knew him at all well. Of course, ordinary photographs of an individual taken from different angles or in different positions shew considerable divergence; perhaps the one approximating nearest to the last photo before transition is the one taken on October 16th, 1921, copy of which I enclose together with print of the pretransitional photograph for comparison. [Not reproduced.—Ed.]

The clearest photo we have had taken of him was on December 11th, 1020.

(*Signed*) FRED J. TWELVES

55, *Victoria Road,*
Whalley Range,
Manchester.

The Testimony of
ALDERMAN W. WHITEFIELD, J.P.,

OF BRISTOL

On August 19th, 1921, I called at Crewe on my way home from Llandudno and made my way to the house

of Mrs. Buxton. I took with me a sealed packet of
plates. I have done a considerable amount of photographic work in days gone by. I examined the camera,
placed the plates into the slides myself in the dark room
and developed and fixed them myself. As regards the
psychic results secured, my good wife and myself have
not the slightest doubt that it is a photograph of one
of our daughters. I do pray that this knowledge may
bring joy and comfort to some sorrowing heart.

(*Signed*) W. WHITEFIELD.

St. George,
Bristol.

An Account of MRS. D. HARTWELL,

OF NORTHAMPTON

(*The photograph referred to by Mrs. Hartwell,*
when compared with a normal photograph of
her late husband, leaves no doubts whatever as
to the question of recognition.)

I went to Mr. Hope as a complete stranger and when
I received the photograph, I recognised the "extra" to
be the likeness of my husband, whom I had lost during
the war. It was also recognised by all of his most intimate friends to whom it was shown.

You have my full permission to make whatever
use of it you wish, and am only too pleased to do anything in my power to help forward this beautiful cause.

(*Signed*) D. HARTWELL.

2, St. Giles Terrace,
Northampton.

[124]

CONCLUSIVE PROOF

An Account by MRS. R. FOULDS,

OF SHEFFIELD

(Mrs. Foulds, an experienced photographer, describes how she obtained a psychic photograph of her mother and a psychograph of more than seventy words, under good test conditions. The psychic photograph showing Mrs. Foulds's mother is reproduced in fig. 24, with normal photograph of the same lady, fig. 25, for comparison.)

The "extra" of my mother (Figure 24) was obtained at 144, Market Street, Crewe, in February, 1920, under the following conditions: I took a sealed packet of plates, also my own slide, which, though slightly different from Mr. Hope's, fitted his camera; after the usual sitting I went into the dark room, broke the seal, opened the packet of plates, placed one in each division of the slide, initialled them, put slide in my dress, also rest of plates, after being focussed I placed slide in camera after a thorough examination of same, resumed my seat, when the usual exposure was made. I then took slide from camera, went into dark room and developed plates, with result that one was normal and the other bore a good likeness of my mother (recognised by all of the family who have seen it). Then Mr. Hope said, "I would like you to choose another plate, any one you like, from your packet, and develop that, too." I chose the one next but one to the bottom of packet, and on developing that, obtained a message of upward of seventy words dealing with matters of a strictly private nature.

[125]

THE CASE FOR SPIRIT PHOTOGRAPHY

I wish to state most emphatically that from beginning to end of the experiment, the packet of plates never left my person, and those developed were not touched in any way whatever by Mr. Hope or Mrs. Buxton until they left the fixing bath, neither did the slide leave my possession except when I placed it in the camera.

(*Signed*) R. FOULDS.

84a, Eastbank Road,
Sheffield.

———

From C. DOVE, ESQ.,

OF SUTTON-IN-ASHFIELD

(In forwarding four psychic photographs with normal photographs for comparison, Mr. Dove gives the attestation hereunder.)

I can absolutely assure you that these photographs were taken under strictest test conditions in my home and in the presence of seven reliable witnesses who are willing to attest to their genuineness.

I myself bought the plates, etc., and was the only one who handled them until they were developed, which was keenly watched by all. Mr. Hope never actually touched the plates. They are fine photographs of Mr. W. J. Cary, Mr. Geo. Dove, of whom there is no normal photo in existence, and Mrs. Catton. I can quite well assure you that they caused quite a sensation in Sutton-in-Ashfield where all of them were well known.

(*Signed*) CHARLES DOVE.

Homelea,
Oak Tree Road,
Sutton-in-Ashfield.

[126]

FIG. 28.—Photograph of Mrs. E. Pickup with psychic likeness of her husband. The sitter was an absolute stranger to the Crewe

FIG. 29.—Photograph of Mrs. Pickup's husband for comparison with his psychic likeness on Fig. 28.

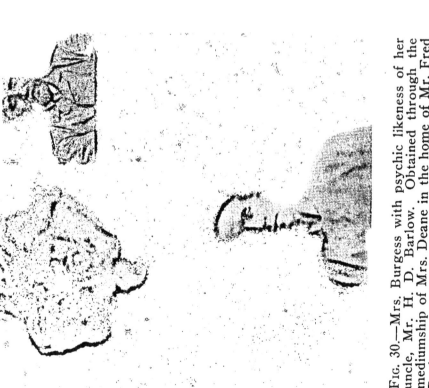

Fig. 30.—Mrs. Burgess with psychic likeness of her uncle, Mr. H. D. Barlow. Obtained through the mediumship of Mrs. Deane in the home of Mr. Fred Barlow, who developed the plate alone in his dark room. An excellent likeness. A normal photograph of Mr. Barlow is shown in the inset. (See p. 63.)

Fig. 31.—Since this book was written, the above important photograph shows that Mr. F. Barlow, in the presence of three witnesses (Messrs. Browne, Newton and Gilby), under good test conditions, obtained through the Crewe Circle a picture of his father. Note how the psychic face has moved and compare with the Deane result (Fig. 30.) and normal photograph. (See inset in Fig. 30.)

CONCLUSIVE PROOF

The Evidence of MRS. A. ELIZABETH GRIERE,

OF DUNFERMLINE

(*The likenesses of father and husband were obtained on one photograph, the features of the latter being clearer than those of the sitter. This photograph is shewn by fig. 26. Fig. 27 reproduced alongside gives a normal photograph of Mr. Griere for comparison.*)

I have great pleasure in forwarding the enclosed pictures. My sitting with Mr. Hope took place in December of 1921. I brought my own plates as directed, and I wish to state that throughout the whole proceedings Mr. Hope did not handle these plates unless to load the camera out in the studio. I took them out of the wrapper, placed them in the slide, unloaded and developed them. The result of the sitting you have before you.

I am perfectly satisfied that the "extra" on No. 1 picture is the face of my husband, and on No. 2 the "extras" are those of my husband and my father. You will see the undoubted resemblance to the original photograph herewith enclosed. *I was a total stranger to Mr. Hope and his good friend, Mrs. Buxton,* and I shall always remain indebted to them both for their courtesy during my visit to Crewe. I trust this picture may be of some use to you.

(*Signed*) A. ELIZABETH GRIERE.

20, *Woodmill Road,*
Dunfermline.

THE CASE FOR SPIRIT PHOTOGRAPHY

The Evidence of E. W. LEE, ESQ.,

OF SHANKLIN, ISLE OF WIGHT

I am enclosing four photographs, one normal and three psychographs. [Not reproduced.—Ed.] All the psychographs were taken in Crewe. Our first meeting was arranged through the post. We were quite strangers and had no mutual acquaintances likely to be in touch with each other. I live in the Isle of Wight; Mr. Hope in Crewe.

The photograph obtained on the first occasion bears the strongest likeness to my dear wife.

The whole operations, less the fixing of the slide in the camera and making the exposure, were undertaken by myself. Although I had not the slightest reason to suspect Mr. Hope, I treated him by my actions as a man open to swindle his patrons.

I am satisfied, bearing in mind that Mr. Hope had not access to any photograph of my wife and following upon the very short time we were together for the first time in our lives, that the result of that sitting could not be produced or attained solely by any *material* means known to mankind, science and legerdemain included.

In June of this year as we were motoring through the country a friend and myself called in Crewe. No appointment had been made with Mr. Hope, but we found him at home. Our dear discarnate friends just before leaving the island on June 4th and June 11th of this year stated they would go with us, and my friend's wife, who had passed over in November, 1921, stated to her husband that he should see her again. To fulfil

[128]

CONCLUSIVE PROOF

this promise we called at Crewe. The small figure at the back is my friend's wife. The other one, if you will compare it with the normal photograph, will not be difficult to identify as my dear wife. On this occasion the features are most sharply defined.

I cannot express my thanks too warmly to the Crewe Circle and my own dear discarnate friends for the trouble taken on our behalf.

(*Signed*) E. W. Lee, Esq.

Fearnside,
Clarence Road,
Isle of Wight.

The Evidence of R. S. HIPWOOD, ESQ.,

OF SUNDERLAND

We lost our only son in France, August 27th, 1918. Being a good amateur photographer, I was curious about the photos that had been taken by the Crewe Circle. We took our own plate with us and I put the plate in the dark slide myself and put my name on it. We exposed two plates in the camera and got a well-recognised photo. Even my nine-year-old grandson could tell who the extra was without anyone saying anything to him. Having a thorough knowledge of photography, I can vouch for the veracity of the photograph in every particular. I claim the print which I send you to be an ordinary photograph of myself and Mrs. Hipwood with the extra of my son, R. W. Hipwood, 13th Welsh Regiment, killed in France in the

THE CASE FOR SPIRIT PHOTOGRAPHY

great advance in August, 1918. I tender to our friends at Crewe our unbounded confidence in their work.

(Signed) R. S. Hipwood.

174, Cleveland Road,
Sunderland.

From LEWIS CHILDS, ESQ.,

OF SHEFFIELD

(This description tells of a compact made between two friends that the one to pass over first should endeavour to manifest to the other. The one friend died, and a few months later Mr. Childs went to Crewe and obtained a fine photograph of his friend, independently recognised by between two hundred and three hundred people who knew him. Mr. Childs' account is accompanied by certificate of recognition from the members of the deceased man's family, who were not spiritualists.)

For five years I worked side by side with Mr. R. H. Turton, and on several occasions tried to interest him in psychic matters by showing him various spirit photographs which I and various friends had secured. He generally greeted the matter contemptuously, and often used the words "bunkum" and "rubbish." On one notable occasion, however, after a long argument, he and I made a compact that which ever of us passed away first should endeavour to give the other some evidence of continued existence beyond death.

Mr. Turton passed away on March 17th of this year. Seven weeks later I visited the Crewe Circle. I made no appointment, and Mr. Hope and Mrs. Bux-

[130]

CONCLUSIVE PROOF

ton could have no idea that I was coming. I took a packet of plates with me and conducted the usual examination of the apparatus used. I opened the box of plates and loaded the carrier. After the exposure had been made I developed and fixed the plate. Everything was in my own hands. As the image came up in the developing dish I noted the face of a man above my right shoulder. The print shows a remarkable likeness to my friend, R. H. Turton, and I am convinced that he has thus fulfilled the compact made betwixt us.

I have shown it to his relatives and friends, and his shopmates, and they have no hesitation in recognising the photograph. Though none of the relatives are spiritualists, they assert that it resembles him as he lay in his coffin. No photograph of Mr. Turton had been taken recently, and I cannot discover one which bears any resemblance to this.

Thus did my friend keep his compact, to convince me that memory lives beyond death.

(*Signed*) L. CHILDS.
42, Glover Road,
Lowfield,
Sheffield.

An Account by MRS. A. A. PEARS,
OF COVENTRY

On returning from our holidays on August 20th, 1918, my husband and myself paid a surprise call at 144, Market Street, Crewe. About three years previously we had lost our little boy of fourteen. None of the members of the Crewe Circle had ever seen him, or

[131]

THE CASE FOR SPIRIT PHOTOGRAPHY

even a photograph of him. On this occasion we were successful in obtaining a wonderful photograph of our dear boy. I have not the least doubt about the reality and genuineness of this photograph. Later on, when in Coventry, Mr. Hope kindly photographed my little boy's grave, and we again obtained a fine photograph of him as he was just before he entered the higher life. With the Crewe Circle I have obtained some remarkable results. No one acquainted with the members of that Circle would for a moment doubt their honesty, and I pray that God may bless and prosper them in their good work and the sacrifices they make for the benefit of their fellows.

(*Signed*) A. A. PEARS.

30, *Dorset Road,*
Coventry.

What reply can be given to such definite statements as these here enumerated by reputable witnesses in every grade of life? Every reader with an open mind will agree that the evidence for the reality of psychic photography is overwhelming. It is only necessary to repeat that these reports form but part of a tremendous mass of accumulated evidence, which is available for any serious student to investigate. Unfortunately, in a popular volume of this description it is possible only to reproduce just a few of the photographic results referred to. As far as possible, however, these photographic effects are being accumulated and preserved so as to form a permanent record of the truth of psychic photography

THE END

CPSIA information can be obtained
at www.ICGtesting.com
Printed in the USA
BVHW090455011118
531857BV00002B/331/P

9 780282 008246